SUMMER SMART

Grade 5·6

Special thanks are given to
Vikalp Jain, **Dev Patel**, **Tiffany Feler**, **Erica Ho**, and **Marco Chang**
for their involvement in the Arts & Crafts Section.

Contents

Mathematics

English

Science

Social Studies

Arts & Crafts

A. **Mrs. Jenkins has 3 triangular flowerbeds. Help her find the perimeter and the angles of each flowerbed. Then write "scalene", "isosceles" or "equilateral" to complete the sentences.**

1.

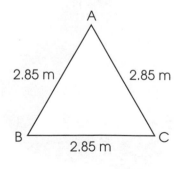

Flowerbed for roses

Perimeter = ___14.6___ m

∠ A = __5__   ∠ B = _____   ∠ C = _____

This flowerbed is in the shape of a / an

___Scalene___ triangle.

2.

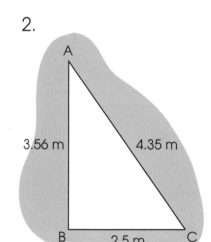

Flowerbed for tulips

Perimeter = _____ m

∠ A = _____   ∠ B = _____   ∠ C = _____

This flowerbed is in the shape of a / an

_____ triangle.

3.

Flowerbed for daisies

Perimeter = _____ m

∠ A = _____   ∠ B = _____   ∠ C = _____

This flowerbed is in the shape of a / an

_____ triangle.

B. **Mrs. Jenkins uses a number line to show how she plants the flowers. Write a decimal number to tell how far each flower is away from the post. Then answer the questions.**

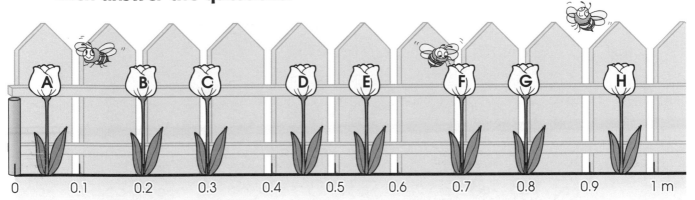

1.   **A** _____ m   **B** _____ m   **C** _____ m   **D** _____ m

     E _____ m   **F** _____ m   **G** _____ m   **H** _____ m

2.   What is the distance between A and B?   _____

3.   What is the distance between D and G?   _____

4.   How many flowers are there within 0.5 m
away from the post?   _____

5.   Describe the rule that Mrs. Jenkins follows to plant her flowers.

_____

C. **Write 2 equivalent fractions to tell what fraction of each set of flowers are pink.**

1.
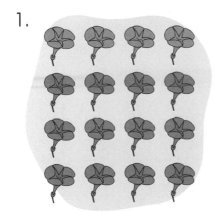

2.
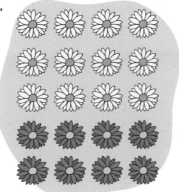

3.
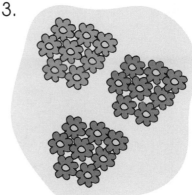

_____ _____   _____ _____   _____ _____

5

Read what the children say. Help them colour the flowers. Then fill in the blanks with fractions to complete the sentences.

1.

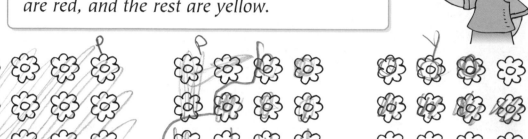

$1\frac{1}{4}$ groups of the flowers are pink, $1\frac{1}{2}$ groups are red, and the rest are yellow.

1_____ of a group of flowers are yellow.

2.

1.2 groups of the flowers are yellow, 0.3 group are red, and the rest are purple.

_____ of a group of flowers are purple.

3.

$\frac{4}{3}$ groups of the flowers are red, $\frac{1}{6}$ group are pink, and the rest are purple.

_____ of a group of flowers are purple.

E. Help Mrs. Jenkins solve the problems.

1. Each flower has 12 petals. 8 flowers have __96__ petals.

2. Each row has 24 flowers. There are __432__ flowers in 18 rows.

3. 5 bags of sunflower seeds weigh 1150 grams. Each bag weighs __230__ g.

4. There are 1275 flowers in the garden. If 865 flowers are red, __410__ flowers are not red.

5. There are 3 flowerbeds with 1275 flowers in the garden. On average, there are __425__ flowers ✗ in each flowerbed.

6. If Mrs. Jenkins waters the flowers with 25.65 L of water every week, she will use __128.25__ L of water in 5 weeks.

 MATH
GAME

Which of the following cubes can be formed from the net on the right? Check ✔ the correct answer.

Ⓐ

Ⓑ ✔

Ⓒ ✗

J. K. Rowling

Is "Rowling" in Magic

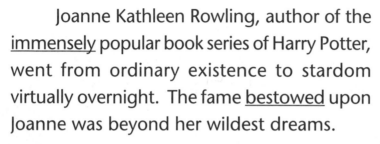

Joanne Kathleen Rowling, author of the <u>immensely</u> popular book series of Harry Potter, went from ordinary existence to stardom virtually overnight. The fame <u>bestowed</u> upon Joanne was beyond her wildest dreams.

Joanne actually came up with the idea for the series in 1990, while sitting on a train in England. Rowling spent the next six years completing the first novel and plotting out the themes of the remaining six books. As a single-parent with little money, Joanne would escape her <u>dismal</u> dwelling with her napping daughter in a baby carriage, and head to a café to write about the Wizard and the "Muggle" worlds.

The first book of the fantasy series, "Harry Potter and the Philosopher's Stone", was published in 1997. It was a <u>smashing</u> success. Since then, J. K. Rowling has nearly produced a sequel every year, with each subsequent book having even darker undertones. However, each story does have the underlying themes of friendship, good conquering evil, and individuality.

J. K. Rowling, presently living in Edinburgh, Scotland, has enjoyed the success of her now established writings. Her books are published in numerous countries around the world and are translated into roughly 30 different languages. As well, film versions have earned rave reviews and the consumer industry has taken off with an endless list of Harry Potter <u>paraphernalia</u>. But, beyond the books, films, and product lines, this fantasy book series has changed the shape of literature and has <u>transcended</u> age groups.

A. **State whether each of the following statements is a fact (F) or an opinion (O).**

1. The Harry Potter series is about the Wizard and the "Muggle" worlds. _____

2. J. K. Rowling went from ordinary existence to stardom overnight. _____

3. "Harry Potter and the Philosopher's Stone" was published in 1997. _____

4. The book was a smashing success. _____

5. J. K. Rowling came up with the idea for the series in 1990. _____

6. At the beginning, J. K. Rowling often wrote in a café. _____

7. The Harry Potter series has been translated into about 30 different languages. _____

8. J. K. Rowling now enjoys her luxurious living in Edinburgh, Scotland. _____

> *When reading an unfamiliar word, it is helpful to use the sentence that the word is in to help understand the meaning. This is called using **context clues**.*

B. **Find these words in the passage and use context clues to determine their meanings. Check with a dictionary when you have finished.**

1. immensely _____

2. bestowed _____

3. dismal _____

4. smashing _____

5. paraphernalia _____

6. transcended _____

C. **Choose the most appropriate noun to complete each sentence below. Make the noun plural before using it.**

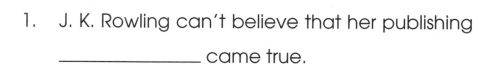

dormitory   dream   class   review
industry   bench   werewolf   country
alley   corridor   potion   life

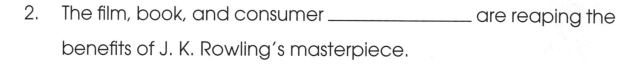

1. J. K. Rowling can't believe that her publishing
    _____ came true.

2. The film, book, and consumer _____ are reaping the
    benefits of J. K. Rowling's masterpiece.

3. The Dursleys' _____ changed when Harry was placed
    on their doorstep.

4. At first, Harry thought _____ were killing the unicorns.

5. The spectators sit on _____ to watch a Quidditch
    match.

6. At night, the Hogwarts students sleep in their _____ .

7. There are many _____ , but only one Diagon Alley.

8. Of all the _____ that Harry takes, he dislikes
    Professor Snape's the most.

9. Professor Snape is responsible for teaching the Hogwarts
    students how to make _____ .

10. There are many _____ leading to the Great Hall.

11. The Harry Potter stories are read by children in different
    _____ all over the world.

12. The film versions of the Harry Potter stories have also earned
    rave _____ .

D. **You have just been asked to interview J. K. Rowling. She has time to answer six questions. Use "How" and the "5 W's of Writing" to compose your well thought-out questions.**

1. How _____

2. Who _____

3. What _____

4. Where _____

5. When _____

6. Why _____

> *Homophones* are words that sound the same, but have different meanings and spellings.

E. **Print the homophone beside each word. Find and circle the new words in the word search.**

l	e	e	r	e	w	l	z	g	w	y	p	r	p	n
z	k	k	r	k	z	m	p	q	e	b	e	o	l	y
q	l	e	l	u	y	x	o	u	x	r	q	u	v	g
e	s	r	a	o	c	n	x	u	a	i	h	t	z	b
k	x	e	b	q	i	b	z	t	r	l	g	e	r	p
u	c	a	o	h	z	w	s	t	t	n	y	f	u	f
k	n	j	l	z	h	v	g	h	s	t	i	j	o	i
d	o	d	p	e	d	b	m	r	n	l	p	n	s	l
n	u	o	t	f	u	x	v	o	g	a	e	f	g	t
o	a	h	p	d	o	t	t	u	r	i	g	h	t	y
w	e	o	e	p	l	c	p	g	u	e	f	x	g	x
r	h	c	r	n	a	j	w	h	i	c	h	y	z	s
i	w	i	a	g	o	p	b	v	a	z	z	x	g	e
b	c	y	c	l	f	w	c	b	n	u	d	r	w	q

grown _____

threw _____

allowed _____

stair _____

course _____

write _____

won _____

morning _____

weather _____

hour _____

witch _____

banned _____

11

ELECTRICITY

Electricity is a form of energy that flows through some materials called conductors. An insulator is a substance that electricity cannot flow through.

A. Check ✔ the pictures that you see evidence of electricity being used.

B. Nicole is looking for a conductor to bridge her circuit so as to make the bulb glow. Help her identify the objects. Write "C" for the conductors or "I" for the insulators.

1. 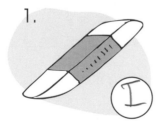 I

2. 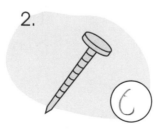 C

3. 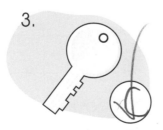 C

4.  I

5.

C. **Mr. Green uses symbols to draw circuit diagrams. Help him identify the symbols with the help of the given words and complete the diagrams.**

cell   bulb   wire   switch

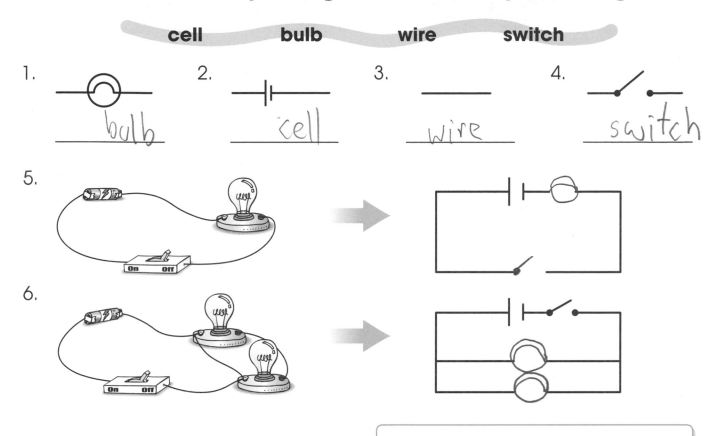

1. bulb
2. cell
3. wire
4. switch

5.

6.

D. **Are the circuits in series or in parallel? Write "series" or "parallel" on the lines.**

Series circuits have one path for electricity to flow along and parallel circuits have more than one path.

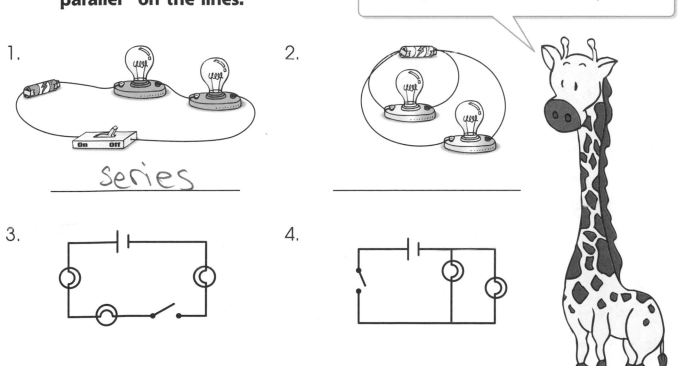

1. series

2. _____

3. _____

4. _____

13

A. Label the provinces and territories on the map below. Colour the province/territory that you live in.

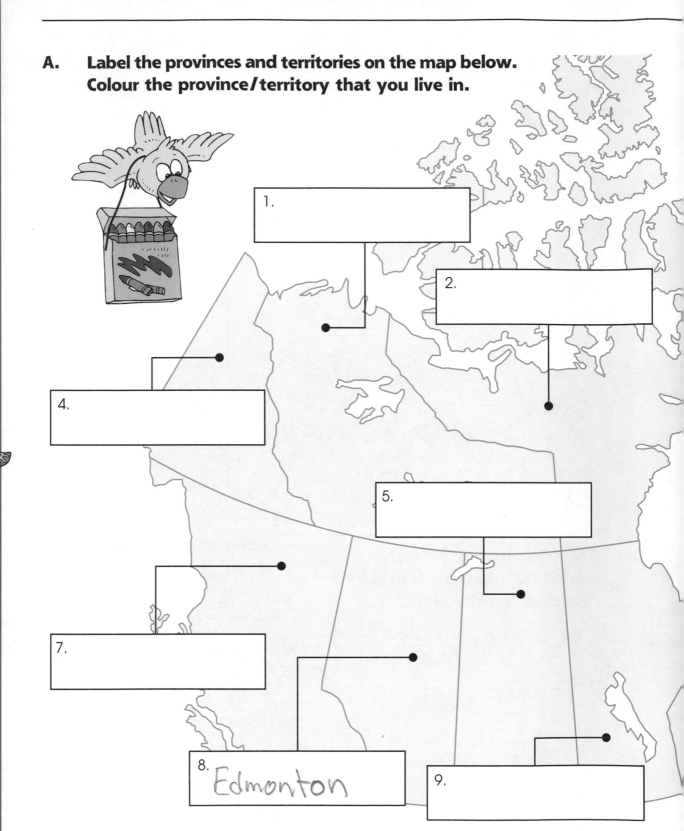

1.

2.

4.

5.

7.

8. Edmonton

9.

B. Write three things special about your province/territory.

1.

2. _____

3. _____

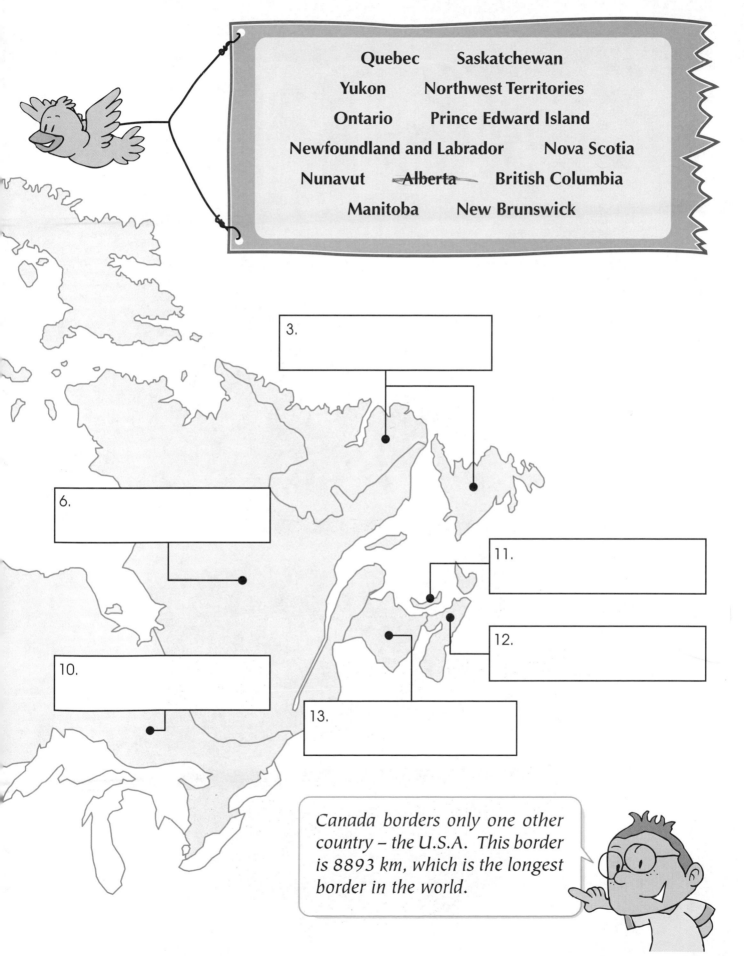

Quebec   Saskatchewan
Yukon   Northwest Territories
Ontario   Prince Edward Island
Newfoundland and Labrador   Nova Scotia
Nunavut   ~~Alberta~~   British Columbia
Manitoba   New Brunswick

3.

6.

11.

10.

12.

13.

Canada borders only one other country – the U.S.A. This border is 8893 km, which is the longest border in the world.

15

GREEK

The Greeks liked decorating their pottery with pictures or patterns.

POTTERY

Materials:

- modelling clay
- newspaper
- paintbrushes
- round balloon
- glaze
- orange, black, and red paint

Directions:

1. Lay newspaper out on work surface.

2. Blow up balloon to size of bowl.

3. Mould clay around the balloon and add handles, lip, etc.

4. Let dry on newspaper – a few days is best.

5. Paint pottery using orange paint. Let dry.

6. Draw design from picture or other source on the pottery piece with black and red paint. Let dry.

7. Using a larger brush, coat pottery with glaze. Let dry.

A. See how much Jimmy saved last week. Help him write the amount he saved each day in decimal and in words. Then answer the questions.

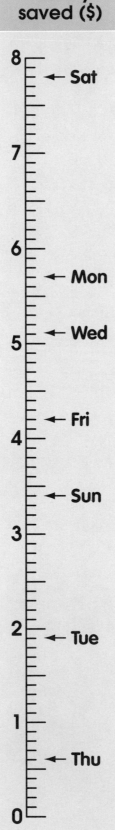

Money saved ($)

1. Sun: $ __3__ ; _____ and _____ hundredths dollar(s)

2. Mon: $ _____ ; _____ dollar(s)

3. Tue: $ _____ ; _____ dollar(s)

4. Wed: $ _____ ; _____ dollar(s)

5. Thu: $ _____ ; _____ dollar(s)

6. Fri: $ _____ ; _____ dollar(s)

7. Sat: $ _____ ; _____ dollar(s)

8. How much did Jimmy save during the weekend? _____

9. How much did Jimmy save from Monday to Friday? _____

10. How much did Jimmy save last week? _____

11. On average, how much did Jimmy save each day? _____

12. If Jimmy trades all his money for $5 bills, how many $5 bills can he get? _____

B. **Look at the things that Jimmy and his dad, Mr. Watts, want to buy for Jimmy's mom. Write the cost of each item. Then solve the problems.**

1.

$ 472.3

2.

$ 177.5

3.

$ 89.26

4.

$ 305.7

5. Which two things cost over $200?

___bracalet___ ; ___camera___

6. The price difference between the cheapest and the most expensive items is $ ___383.04___

7. If Jimmy and his dad share equally the cost for a bottle of perfume, each of them needs to pay $ ___44.63___ .

C. **Benny's Store is having a sale and all the prices include taxes. Each customer can pick one card below to see how much he can save. Help Jimmy solve the problems.**

Cashier

Lucky Box

1. What is the probability that Jimmy will pick a

 ?

1/8

2. What is the probability that he will pick a ?

1/4

3. What is the probability that he will pick a ?

0/0

4. What is the probability that he will pick a card to save more than $9.99?

1/0

5. The item that Jimmy wants to buy costs $89.66.

a. If Jimmy picks a 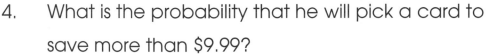 , how much does he need to pay?

85.66

b. If Jimmy and his dad each pay $39.83, which card does Jimmy pick?

D. **Darren and Eva are counting their coins to pay for their purchases. See how they put the coins into groups. Help them fill in the missing numbers.**

1.

There are 4 loonies in a group.

a. __1__ x \$4 = \$4   b. __2__ x \$4 = \$8   c. __3__ x \$4 = \$12

d. __4__ x \$4 = \$16   e. __5__ x \$4 = \$20   f. _____ x \$4 = \$28

g. __8__ x \$4 = \$32   h. __9__ x \$4 = \$36   i. _____ x \$4 = \$40

2.

There are 3 toonies in a group.

a. __1__ x \$6 = \$6   b. __2__ x \$6 = \$12   c. _____ x \$6 = \$18

d. __3__ x \$6 = \$24   e. __5__ x \$6 = \$30   f. _____ x \$6 = \$36

g. __7__ x \$6 = \$42   h. _____ x \$6 = \$48   i. _____ x \$6 = \$54

BRAIN TEASER

Jimmy put 3 identical rolls of coins into a tank filled with water. See how much water was displaced. Help Jimmy find the volume of each roll of coins.

The volume of each roll of coins is

_____ cm^3.

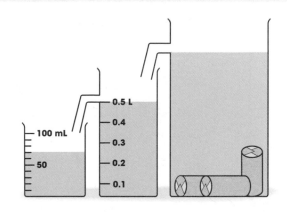

21

Scream Machines

Roller coasters have certainly evolved over the ages. The first roller coasters appeared in Russia in the 16th century. They were called "scream machines". These roller coasters were simply wooden sleds that journeyed down a five-storey, ice-packed hill in the winter.

In the 19th century, small wheels were attached to the bottoms of these sleds. However, no emphasis was placed on safety and, as a result, many people were injured with carts flying off the tracks. But, as years passed, improvements were made in the areas of track, locking wheels, and lift cables for the cars.

By the end of the 1800s, circular loop rides had emerged and amusement parks became popular. However, when the Great Depression struck in 1929, people lost their jobs and had no money for leisure activities. The amusement park industry was in dire straits.

In 1955, Walt Disney brought a remarkable change to the business when he opened Disneyland in California. Before long, theme parks were opening again and a variety of roller coaster designs were created.

Today, the latest in roller coasters can reach incredible speeds of approximately 190 kilometres per hour, heights and drops of roughly 120 metres, track lengths as far as 850 metres, and angles of ascents and descents up to 90 degrees.

Regardless of the type of roller coaster, it is obvious from the sounds and faces of the riders that a different sensation is created for each individual. Some have the look of shock, as though they have just seen a ghost, others look like their stomach has been invaded by an alien, and yet others are laughing uncontrollably, like they've had the time of their lives. Which is it for you?

A. **Find in the passage the effect of each of the following.**

1. In the 16th century, Russians journeyed down an ice-packed hill on wooden sleds.

   Effect: _____

2. No emphasis was placed on the safety of the scream machines.

   Effect: _____

3. Circular loop rides emerged in the 1800s.

   Effect: _____

4. During the Great Depression, people lost their jobs.

   Effect: _____

5. Walt Disney opened Disneyland in 1955.

   Effect: _____

   _____

B. **Match the words in the passage with their meanings.**

1.	evolved	_____	A.	importance
2.	century	_____	B.	moving upwards
3.	emphasis	_____	C.	position of difficulty
4.	emerged	_____	D.	a physical feeling
5.	dire straits	_____	E.	one hundred years
6.	ascents	_____	F.	came into existence
7.	descents	_____	G.	going downwards
8.	sensation	_____	H.	developed

C. **In the following sentences, circle the proper nouns and underline the common nouns.**

1. Cedar Point and Six Flags Magic Mountain are among the leading roller coaster amusement parks in the world.

2. The cost of building just one roller coaster is well into the millions of dollars.

3. One of the scientific principles of how roller coasters move is based on gravity, which was discovered by Sir Isaac Newton.

4. The new ride at Cedar Point, called "Top Thrill Dragster", opened in May of 2003.

5. Six Flags Magic Mountain launched their new ride called "Scream" in the Spring of 2003.

6. "The Supreme Scream" is one of the world's tallest freefall rides at over 30 storeys high.

D. **Combine the following pairs of sentences to form complex sentences.**

1. The first roller coasters appeared in Russia in the 16th century. They were called "scream machines".

   _____

   _____

2. The Great Depression struck in 1929. The amusement park industry was forced to close down.

   _____

   _____

3. People enjoy riding on roller coasters. They derive a lot of excitement from the rides.

   _____

   _____

E.   **Roller Coaster Trivia – Circle the correct answers.**

1.   The amusement park industry went downhill because of
   A.   World War I.   B.   lack of lumber.
   C.   the Great Depression.

2.   The latest in roller coasters has angles of ascents and descents
   A.   up to 90 degrees.   B.   up to 60 degrees.
   C.   more than 90 degrees.

3.   The first roller coasters appeared in
   A.   Asia.   B.   Russia.   C.   Canada.

4.   The first roller coasters were
   A.   sleds on tracks.   B.   sleds.   C.   sleds with wheels.

5.   Walt Disney was credited for
   A.   reviving theme parks.
   B.   building monster roller coasters.
   C.   improved safety on roller coasters.

> *Persuasive writing* gives an opinion and tries to convince the reader to agree with that opinion by using facts and examples.

F.   **Write a letter to your parents persuading or convincing them to let you go on the fastest, highest, scariest roller coaster in the world.**

E N E R G Y

Energy is the ability to make things move. Moving things do work. Energy comes in many forms. One is kinetic energy. Kinetic energy is the energy possessed by anything that is moving.

A. What type of energy can you see in the picture?

| elastic | light | sound | gravitational |
| kinetic | chemical | heat | electrical |

1.

2.

3.

4.

5.

6.

7.

8.

B. **Choose, from the three listed energy forms, the result of each energy transformation.**

kinetic   heat   light

Energy In	Transformer	Energy Out

1. electrical _____

2. chemical _____

3. potential _____

4. chemical _____ ,

_____

5. chemical _____ ,

_____

C. **Identify the type of energy transformation in each situation.**

1. The poles of the battery were bridged with a strip of aluminum foil.

_____ energy to _____ energy

2. About 10 mL of vinegar was placed into a film canister, with some baking soda added and the lid snapped on tight.

_____ energy to _____ energy

A. Complete the following tree diagram on the federal government with the correct terms.

Structure of the Federal Government

Prime Minister   Parliament
House of Commons   Ministries and Civil Service
Provincial Courts   Federal Courts   Sovereign
Governor General   Supreme Court   Cabinet   Senate

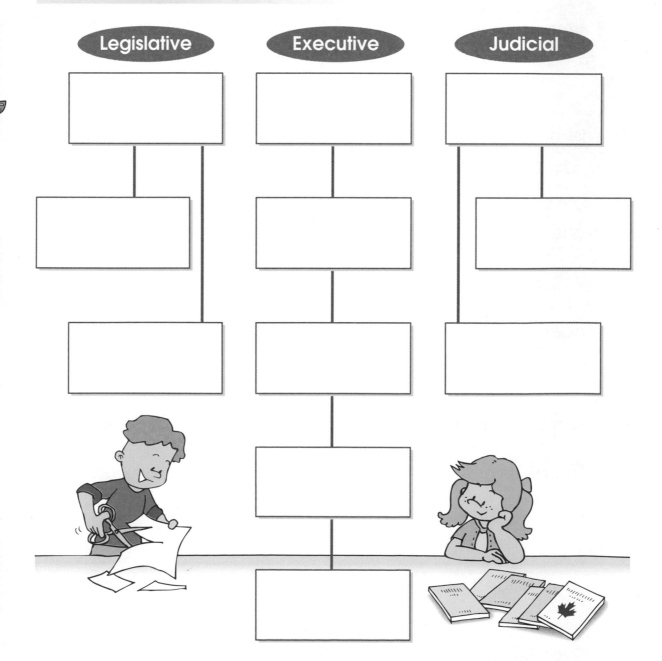

B.   Find out some information about the province/territory you live in.

1.   Province/Territory: _____

2.   Capital City: _____

3.   Lieutenant Governor/Commissioner: _____

4.   Premier/Government Leader: _____

5.   Member of Legislative Assembly representing you:

_____

C.   Draw the flag of your province/territory in the space below and write what it symbolizes.

On February 15, 1995, Prime Minister Jean Chrétien proclaimed that every February 15 be known as Flag Day, to commemorate the first time the maple leaf flag was raised over Parliament Hill 30 years before that.

GREEK Statue

A

Materials:

- small block of wood (4 cm x 10 cm)
- 2 small nails (wide heads)
- small container of water
- wooden popsicle sticks
- modelling clay
- hammer
- thin wire
- toothpicks
- pliers
- wire cutter

Directions:

1. Form body using wire and nail it onto wood piece, as in A .

2. Press clay into and around the wire body, making arms, legs, torso, etc., as in B .

3. Cover nails in feet with clay on wood.

4. Dip fingers in water and smooth out body parts.

5. Use popsicle stick and toothpick to carve out the features of statue. Use water to smooth over features.

6. Use toothpicks to make eyes, mouth, brows, ears, etc.

7. Cover wooden block with clay.

8. Finito!!!

A. Louis has a fast food shop. Look at the price list and read what Louis says. Help him write the prices of the combos.

Price List

Hamburger	$3.59	Fries	$1.96	Coffee	$1.42
Hot dog	$2.59	Pie	$1.98	Tea	$1.29
Sandwich	$3.69	Sundae	$2.09	Pop	$0.99

Each combo is $1.88 cheaper than the food and drink ordered separately.

A

$ 5.88

B

$ 4.01

C

$ 4.60

D

$

E

$

F

$

Week
3

MATHEMATICS

B.   Louis is preparing the food. Help him solve the problems.

1.

Each box of burgers costs $9.97. How much do 5 boxes of burgers cost?

_____ = _____ $ _____

2.

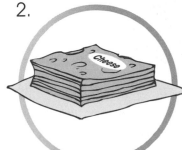

A package of cheese weighs 1.45 kg. How many kilograms do 3 packages of cheese weigh?

_____ = _____   _____ kg

3.

A bag has 12 cookies. How many cookies are there in 16 bags?

_____ = _____   _____ cookies

4.

A bag of chips weighs 38 g. How heavy is a box of 12 bags of chips?

_____ = _____   _____ g

5.

The weight of 3 packages of sausages are 885 g, 1248 g, and 1682 g. What is the total weight of these 3 packages of sausages?

_____ = _____   _____ g

C. Each customer can spin one of the spinners below to get a free food item. Help Louis measure the angles of each sector. Then answer the questions.

1.

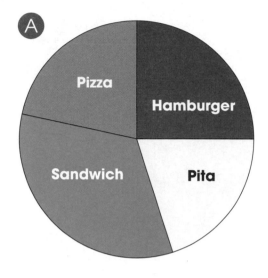

2.

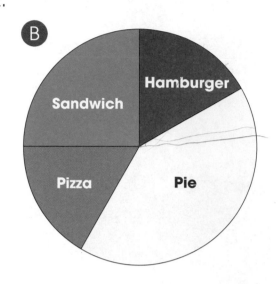

	Angle of Each Sector
Hamburger	equal
Pita	interior
Sandwich	superior
Pizza	interior

	Angle of Each Sector
Hamburger	interion
Pie	superior
Sandwich	equal
Pizza	interior

3. What are the possible outcomes of Spinner A?

   Pizza, pita, sandwich and hamburger

4. What are the possible outcomes of Spinner B?

   the same

5. What is the probability that Spinner A will land on "Hamburger"?   1/4

6. What is the probability that Spinner B will land on "Pizza"?   0.6/4

D. Help Louis make a bar graph and a pictograph to show what kind of food the customers got from each spinner.

Food the Customers Got from Spinning Spinner A

Type of Food	Number
Hamburger	100
Pita	80
Sandwich	120
Pizza	85

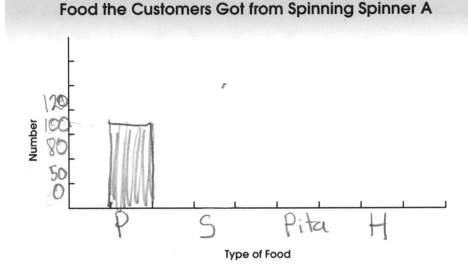

Food the Customers Got from Spinning Spinner B

Each picture = 10

Type of Food	Number
Hamburger	45
Pie	100
Pizza	45
Sandwich	60

BRAIN TEASER

Look at the graphs above. Answer Louis's question.

The graphs show how much food was given out from January 27 to the last day of January. What was the average number of food items given out each day?

The average was _____ .

A. **Nicole forgot to use paragraphs in her letter. Read the letter and put the paragraph symbol "¶" before each sentence where a new paragraph is needed. (Hint: There are six paragraphs.)**

Back to *Nature*

July 10

Dear Mom and Dad,

Adriana and I are having a fantastic time at Uncle Ross and Aunt Joyce's. It is like a paradise here, with an overlooking view of the water called "Satellite Channel" (not the television kind, Dad). I'm learning to have a real appreciation for wildlife and the outdoors. Yesterday, while on route on the charter plane from Vancouver to Victoria, we were amazed to spot a pod of approximately 20 orcas, their dorsal fins piercing the water each time they surfaced. It was an incredible sight! Did you know that pods of the resident killer whales are made up of the mother's immediate and extended family members? They may stay together as a family even after they're fully grown and can live anywhere from 50 to 80 years. Today, we saw a number of sea lions and otters frolicking in the water. It seemed quite peculiar to see this one otter lying on its back; it had a stone on its belly and a scallop in its paw. We discovered afterward that otters actually float on their backs while they crack open the seashell of their prey with a rock. You won't believe this – there's a pair of bald eagles nesting in Aunt Joyce and Uncle Ross's very own backyard. It's astounding to see the eagles swooping in at speeds of up to 160 kilometres per hour over the water for their daily fish catch. The term "eagle eyes" is no joke. They can spot fish at distances of about 1.5 km away. Aunt Joyce doesn't mind the eagles hanging out in their fir trees, but she does get frustrated with the deer and rabbits that frequent their grounds. These sneaky vegetarians arrive after dusk, having already eaten their main meal in nearby fields, only to enjoy Aunt Joyce's roses and lilies for their dessert. I guess they feel comfortable trespassing on the property, since there is no dog to frighten them off. Tomorrow, Uncle Ross is taking us on an excursion to Johnstone Strait, where he's confident that we will sight a pod or two of orcas. Apparently in July and August, the number of whales in this area peaks, due to salmon passing through (one of their favourite foods). They naturally make this one of their main foraging territories. I'll give you more details when I get home.

Love,

Nicole

P.S. Adriana is a bit homesick.

B.   State whether each of the following statements is a fact (F) or an opinion (O).

1.   _____   One way to travel from Vancouver to Victoria is by charter plane.

2.   _____   Bald eagles can see up to a distance of 1.5 kilometres.

3.   _____   Many orcas inhabit Johnstone Strait during the salmon season.

4.   _____   Uncle Ross and Aunt Joyce's house is like a holiday resort.

5.   _____   Deer and rabbits only get hungry after dusk.

6.   _____   Killer whales live in pods and can live up to 80 years.

7.   _____   Otters may use rocks to crack open hard-shell prey.

8.   _____   You need to go to Victoria, B.C. if you want to truly experience animals in their natural habitats.

C.   Answer the following questions.

1.   "It was an incredible sight!" What did Nicole see?

_____

_____

2.   "The term 'eagle eyes' is no joke." Why did Nicole make this remark?

_____

_____

3.   What were "these sneaky vegetarians"?

_____

_____

4.   "They naturally make this one of their main foraging territories." What do "they" and "this" refer to?

_____

_____

D. **Read the clues and complete the crossword puzzle with words from the passage.**

Across

A. secretive

B. amazing

C. unusual, strange

D. unbelievable

E. searching for food

Down

1. diving

2. back

3. moving lively

4. go regularly to a place

ENGLISH

E. **Read the following sentences. Write "A" for sentences in the active voice and "P" for sentences in the passive voice.**

1. The otter cracked open the shell of a scallop with a rock. _____

2. The scallop was eaten by the otter. _____

3. The dog scared the deer away. _____

4. The deer was scared away by the dog. _____

5. I was caught by surprise! _____

6. We went from Vancouver to Victoria by charter plane. _____

F. **Rewrite the following sentences by changing them from active voice to passive or from passive to active.**

1. The bald eagle spotted a big fish.

_____

2. Uncle Ross took us to the shore in his van.

_____

_____

3. A pod of orcas was seen by Nicole and Adriana.

_____

_____

4. We were reminded by the warden to be careful.

_____

_____

5. Aunt Joyce prepared a hearty meal for us.

_____

Force & Structure

> A **force** is a push or pull that results when an object interacts with another object. Forces occur in pairs.

A. Identify the pairs of forces acting upon the objects that are interacting. Draw arrows to show the directions of the action and reaction forces.

reaction

action

reaction

reaction

B. Complete the sentences with the help of the word bank.

| inclined plane | torque | Newton | spoke |

1. Metre is to length as _____ is to force.

2. _____ is to jar lid as pull is to cork.

3. Beam is to bridge as _____ is to bicycle wheel.

4. Lever is to see-saw as _____ is to playground slide.

C. **Let's do this activity. Design and construct a structure that will protect your egg from any accidental falls.**

Build a structure with the listed materials to protect an egg. When completed, it should be able to survive a drop of up to 2 metres off the floor.

Here is a list! You do not have to use all of the materials, but you must use only those on the list.

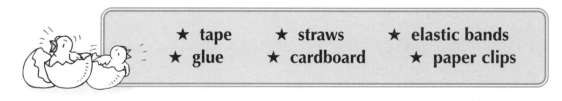

| ★ tape | ★ straws | ★ elastic bands |
| ★ glue | ★ cardboard | ★ paper clips |

Here's a place to sketch out your plan. Design it. Build it. Test it.

41

A. The Greeks were well-known as thinkers and philosophers. Read the words and clues. Complete the crossword puzzle.

Across

A. the country of which Alexander was king
B. Alexander became this at the age of 13.
C. the study of the way things really are
D. All the five major schools of ancient Greece were affected by his thinking.

Down

1. This book was about an ideal society.
2. He founded the Academy, the world's first "university".
3. "Ruled by the People"
4. He was the tutor of Alexander the Great.
5. the city Alexander the Great built

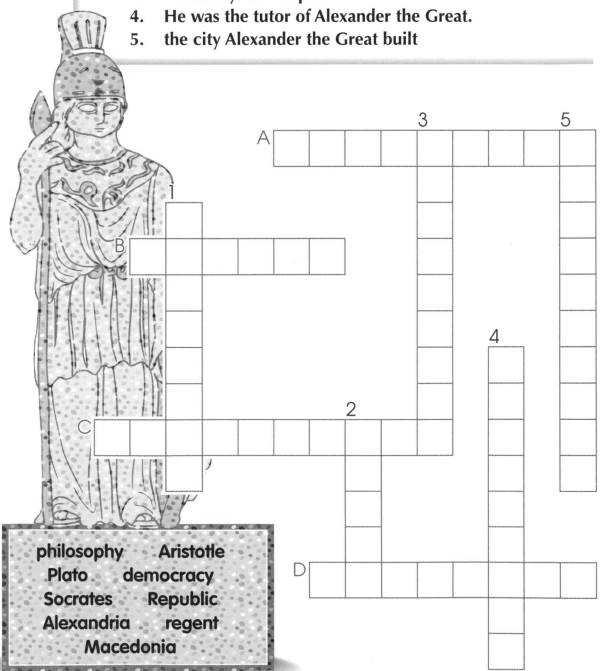

philosophy   Aristotle
Plato   democracy
Socrates   Republic
Alexandria   regent
Macedonia

B. **Use the Greek alphabet to decode the statements below.**

A – alpha	a		I – iota	i		P – rho	r
B – beta	b		K – kappa	k		Σ – sigma	s
Γ – gamma	g		Λ – lambda	l		T – tau	t
Δ – delta	d		M – mu	m		Υ – upsilon	u,y
E – epsilon	e		N – nu	n		Φ – phi	ph
Z – zeta	z		Ξ – i	x		X – chi	ch
H – eta	e		O – omicron	o		Ψ – psi	ps
Θ – theta	th		Π – pi	p		Ω – omega	w

1. ΑΘΕΝΣ ΙΣ ΝΑΜΕΔ fΟΡ ΑΘΕΝΑ, ΘΕ ΓΟΔΔΕΣΣ Οf ΩΙΣΔΟΜ.

    _____

2. ΓΡΕΕΚΣ ΤΟΟΚ ΟνΕΡ ΑΤΤΙcΑ ΙΝ 1900 B.C. ΑΝΔ ΘΕ ΝΑΜΕ ΒΕcΑΜΕ
    ΑΘΕΝΣ.

    _____

    _____

3. ΑΘΕΝΣ ΔΕfΕΑΤΕΔ ΠΕΡΣΙΑ ΑΝΔ ΒΕcΑΜΕ ΑΝ ΕΜΠΙΡΕ.

    _____

About 12% of our words come from the Greek alphabet.

Scarab

Paperweight

Materials:

- smooth, round beach stone
- pencil
- blue and white paint
- small, thin paintbrush
- wide paintbrush
- glaze

Directions:

1. Wash and dry small stone.

2. Draw outlines as shown, using pencil.

3. Paint scarab. Let dry.

4. Draw outlines again with white paint. Let dry.

5. Paint over stone with glaze. Let dry.

A. **The children cut a letter from each piece of cardboard. Help them find the area of each letter and answer the questions.**

1. Eli cut the letters E, L, and I.

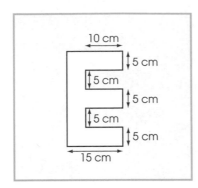 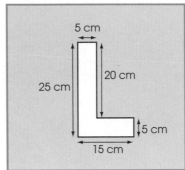 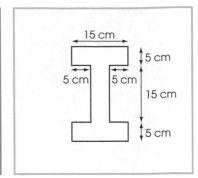

_____ cm²   _____ cm²   _____ cm²

2. If Eli puts a string around the border of each letter, what will the length of that string be?

_____ cm

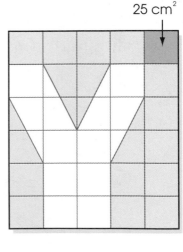

3. Amy cut the letters A, M, and Y.

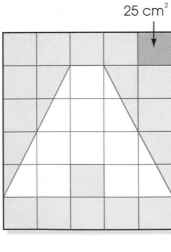 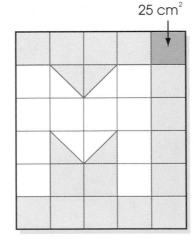 

_____ cm²   _____ cm²   _____ cm²

4. A roll of lace is 1 m long. If Amy needs 785 cm to add lace borders to her letters, how many rolls of lace does she need?   _____ roll(s)

B. **See how many letters each child cut. Read what they say. Write the letters in the boxes. Then fill in the blanks.**

1.

3 tenths of the letters I cut are A, 25 hundredths are M, and the rest are Y.

a.

A	A	A	A	A	A	A	A	A	A
A	A	A	A	A	A	A	A	A	A
A	A	A	A	A	A	A	A	A	A

b.   Write a fraction and a decimal number that tell how many letters Amy cut are Y.

_____ ; _____

2.

0.05 of the letters I cut are T, 0.2 are O, 0.35 are N, and the rest are Y.

a.

b.   Write a fraction and a decimal number that tell how many letters Tony cut are Y.

_____ ; _____

47

C. See how the children built their names with 1-cm³ cubes. Help them find the volume of each letter. Then write 2 equivalent fractions to tell what part of each letter is coloured and answer the questions.

1.

Letter	Volume (cm³)	Coloured Part
E		
L		
I		
T		
O		
N		
Y		

2. How many cubes did Eli use to build his name? _____

3. What fraction of the cubes that Eli used are coloured? _____

D. **The children drew some letters. Measure the angle of each of their letters and draw a congruent letter with the given line.**

1.

_____

2.

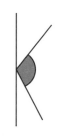 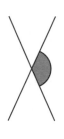 

_____

3.

_____

4.

_____

BRAIN TEASER

The children cut 360 letters in all and used a circle graph to show the quantity of each type of letter. Answer their questions.

Number of Letters with Different Patterns

1. What fraction of the letters have dots? _____

2. How many letters have dots? _____

3. What fraction of the letters have stripes? _____

4. How many letters have stripes? _____

5. How many letters have checks? _____

Tony Hawk
Soars in Success

When you hear the words "ollie", "nose grind", "kick flip", "fakie", "900", "mongo-foot", and "McTwist", what comes to mind – a new language perhaps? Actually, these are just a few of the many skateboarding terms used to describe skateboarder tricks.

Skateboarding has been around since the early 1900s, but it was very different from the skateboarding of today, now deemed an "extreme sport". Skateboarding falls into this classification mainly because of the daredevil aerial stunts that are performed while skidding onto and over obstacles at astonishing speeds.

For most people, skateboarding is a recreational activity, but there are some that take it to a higher level and make a career out of it. Tony Hawk is one of them. Tony Hawk, a world leader in skateboarding, became a professional at the young age of 14, with the unconditional support of his family. In fact, Tony's father founded the National Skateboarding Association (now called World Cup Skateboarding).

Hawk is most legendary for being the first to do the "900", which is two and a half rotations above the half-pipe. He successfully landed this trick at the "X Games" in 1999. Since he started competing over 20 years ago, Tony has won numerous titles, and is a thirteen-time medallist at the "X Games".

Now, in his mid-30s, Tony doesn't compete anymore, but he still skateboards and continues to be involved in the sport. He is featured in commercials, films, and magazines, and has his own signature video game and skateboard clothing line. At skateboarding events, he interviews the athletes and does commentary. Hawk has established the Tony Hawk Foundation, a non-profit charitable organization to help subsidize the building of public skateboard parks across the United States.

A.   Answer the following questions.

1.   Why is skateboarding regarded as an "extreme sport"?

_____

_____

2.   What shows that Hawk had the full support of his family in doing skateboarding?

_____

3.   Explain what "900" is in skateboarding.

_____

4.   List two ways by which Hawk is still involved in skateboarding.

_____

_____

5.   What is the Tony Hawk Foundation for?

_____

_____

**B.   Unscramble the letters to create words about skateboarding.
(Hint: All of the words can be found in the passage.)**

1.   teermex   _____

2.   epotcem   _____

3.   ntsust   _____

4.   leoli   _____

5.   esslcoabt   _____

6.   rbsktoaead   _____

C. Select the statement "A" or "B" that best describes the main idea for each paragraph from the passage.

Paragraph One

A. Tony Hawk speaks a foreign language.
B. Skateboarders have interesting words to describe their tricks.

Paragraph Two

A. The sport of skateboarding has changed over the years to become an extreme sport.
B. Extreme sports have an element of danger about them.

Paragraph Three

A. Tony Hawk has taken skateboarding to a higher level.
B. One can become a professional athlete at the age of 14.

Paragraph Four

A. Tony Hawk is a hero.
B. Tony Hawk has had a successful skateboarding career.

Paragraph Five

A. Tony Hawk enjoys being involved with various aspects of the media.
B. Although Tony Hawk is no longer a competitor, he is active in keeping the sport alive.

D. Look at the verbs below. Classify each as an action, saying, or thinking/feeling verb. Write them on the lines below.

wonder	exclaim	rotate	believe
glide	applaud	whisper	ask	amaze

Action Verb	Saying Verb	Thinking / Feeling Verb
_____	_____	_____
_____	_____	_____
_____	_____	_____

E. **Write a descriptive paragraph on what it would be like to participate in an extreme sport that you have never tried, but always wanted to.**

Skateboarding is one of many "Extreme Sports". Some others include: snowboarding, mountain biking, motocross, BMX biking, in-line skating, street luge, parasailing, and skydiving.

*A **descriptive paragraph** describes a topic in such detail using the five senses that the reader actually feels that they are right there with you.*

_____

_____

_____

_____

_____

_____

_____

_____

_____

_____

_____

53

Human Body Systems

A. **Look at the labelled containers. Help Dr. Frank write the words in the word bank on the appropriate containers.**

trachea   cartilage   gall bladder   capillary   bone   bronchiole
ligament   vein   cerebrum   salivary gland
cerebellum   artery   bronchus   optic nerve   esophagus

Skeletal System

Circulatory System

Nervous System

Respiratory System

Digestive System

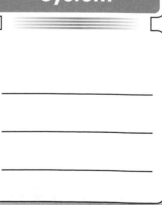

B. **Identify which body part does the job. Complete the chart with the words from the word bank.**

white blood cell   spinal cord   skin   muscle   kidney   lung   stomach

Human Body Part	Form and Function
_____	organ where gastric juices help break down food
_____	the brain communicates with the nerves through this
_____	cleans the blood and gets rid of waste material
_____	tissue that works with bone to make the body move
_____	keeps water from getting in and fluids from leaving the body
_____	organ through which we get oxygen
_____	found in the blood that fights infection

C. **Choose the correct number for each fact.**

350   12   46   206   5   72

1. Number of bones you are born with: _____

2. Number of millions of hairs you have: _____

3. Number of pairs of ribs in the human body: _____

4. Number of chromosomes in each human cell: _____

5. Number of bones you have when you are an adult: _____

6. Number of muscles used to speak a single word: _____

A. Read this passage about the Mayans. Fill in the blanks.

specific   farming   home   cooking
astronomy   traded   pyramids   1200   500
fields   temples   palaces   mathematics   food
hieroglyphics   conflicts   climate   collapse
archaeological   temples   tombs   Mexico

The Mayans were 1._____ people. Like many early civilizations, men and women had 2._____ roles. The men and boys were responsible for working the 3._____ while the women and girls were responsible for 4._____ and tending the 5._____ .

Even in these early times (6._____ B.C.E.), the Mayans 7._____ goods for other items they needed. Later in 8._____ B.C.E., the Mayans began to develop cities. They built 9._____ , 10._____ , and 11._____ . The Mayans expanded their knowledge of 12._____ and 13._____ and developed a system of writing known as 14._____ .

The Mayans had many achievements, some of which are visible today through the 15._____ discoveries. Several 16._____ and 17._____ have been discovered, particularly in 18._____ .

There may be several reasons for the 19._____ of the Mayan civilizations. One of these may have been the 20._____ among cities. Also 21._____ changes and 22._____ shortages may have contributed to their downfall.

B. **Try and complete the chart showing the Maya numbers from zero to nineteen.**

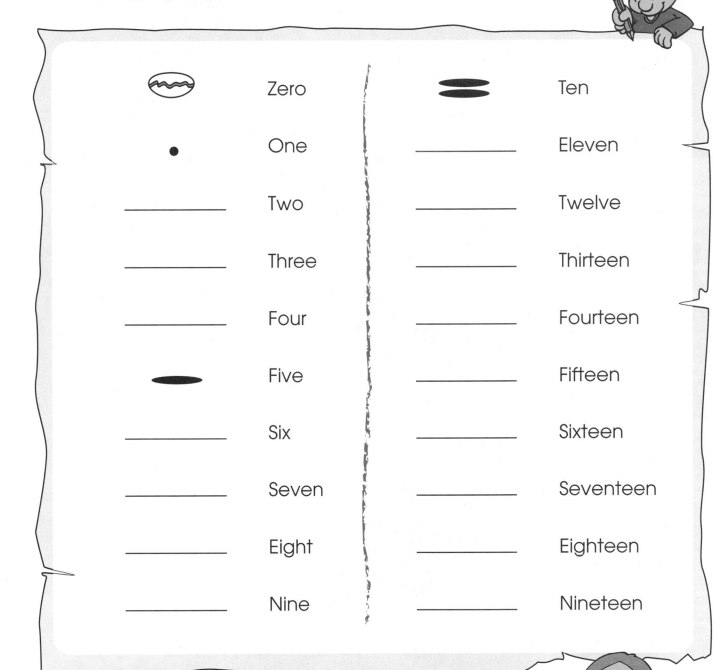

⬭	Zero	▬	Ten
•	One	_____	Eleven
_____	Two	_____	Twelve
_____	Three	_____	Thirteen
_____	Four	_____	Fourteen
▬	Five	_____	Fifteen
_____	Six	_____	Sixteen
_____	Seven	_____	Seventeen
_____	Eight	_____	Eighteen
_____	Nine	_____	Nineteen

Did you know? The Mayans are credited with the creation and use of the number zero.

Make a mathematical sentence using the Maya numbers and test it on your friend.

_____

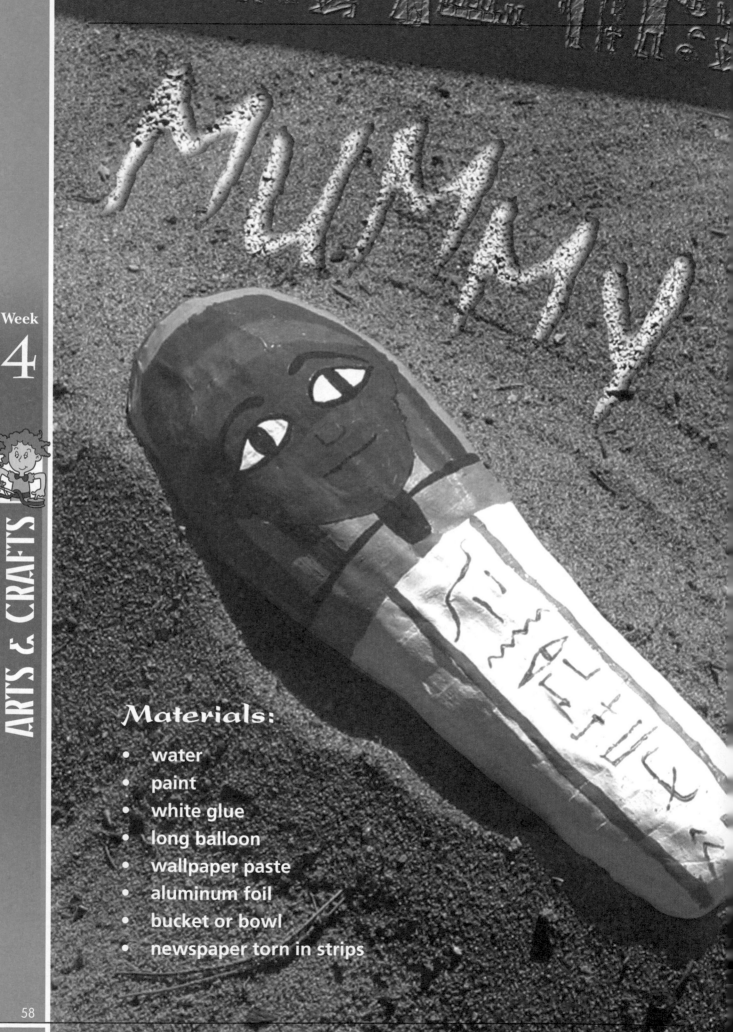

ARTS & CRAFTS

MUMMY

Materials:

- water
- paint
- white glue
- long balloon
- wallpaper paste
- aluminum foil
- bucket or bowl
- newspaper torn in strips

Directions:

1. Mix paste and water until mixture has consistency of sour cream.

2. Blow up balloon and tie; wrap aluminum foil around balloon.

3. Dip strips of newspaper into wallpaper paste.

4. Wrap strips around "mummy" until it looks like the shape of mummy. Let dry.

5. Seal case with coat of white glue. Let dry.

6. Paint mummy case and draw traditional mask.

A. **Look at the flyer. Help Toysland's owner, Mrs. Jenkins, write the sale price of each item in the**  **.**

Sale

$10 – $30	**$4.50 OFF**
$30.01 – $60	**$9.99 OFF**
over $60	**$25.59 OFF**

Toysland

Sun - Sat   9:00 a.m. - 9:00 p.m.

Regular $28.56

Regular $35.49

Regular $99.99

Board Game

Puzzle

Sale $ 26.50

Sale $ 30

Sale $ 50

Regular $59.97

Sale $

Sale $

Regular $19.99

Sale $

Regular $32.97

B. See how the people pay for their toys. Help Mrs. Jenkins solve the problems.

1. Linda buys 2 boxes of puzzles. What is her change from a $100 bill?

   Her change is $ _70_ .

2. Tom buys a box of board game and a laptop. What is his change from 4 $20 bills?

   His change is $ _____ .

3. Mr. Venn buys a racing car and a teddy bear. What is his change from 2 $50 bills?

   His change is $ _____ .

4. Jennie pays for a guitar with a $10 bill, a $5 bill, and 4 loonies. How much more money does she need?

   She needs $ _____ more.

C. Help Mrs. Jenkins match the nets with the gift boxes and complete the table.

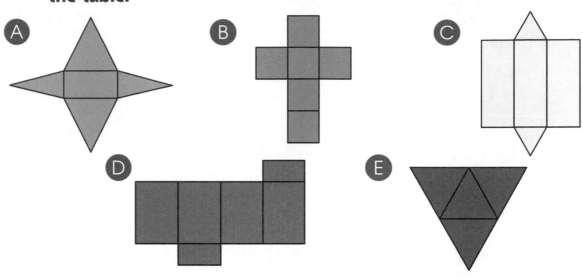

Gift Box	Net	Name of Shape	Number of Faces	Number of Vertices
1.				
2.				
3.				
4.				
5.				

D. See how Mrs. Jenkins put her toys. Help her write the coordinates and solve the problems.

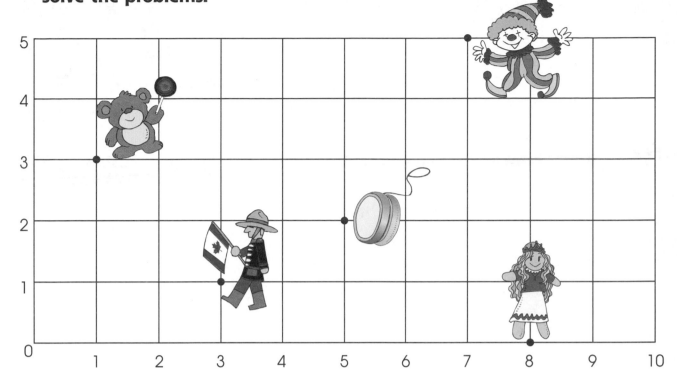

1. The coordinates of

    Bear (,   )   Yo-yo (,   )   Doll (,   )

2. The bear is _____ unit(s) left / right and _____ unit(s) up / down from the origin.

3. The RCMP is _____ unit(s) left / right and _____ unit(s) up / down from the clown.

MATH GAME

Solve the problems.

Mr. Moxam bought 13 boxes of puzzles and board games for $166. If each box of puzzle cost $12.50 and each box of board game cost $13, how many boxes of puzzles did he buy?

He bought _____ boxes of puzzles.

63

How Do You Catch a Dream?

It is a Native American legend that a dream catcher can help to stop nightmares or bad dreams. Ancestors of Native Americans made the frame of the dream catcher from red willow wood twisted into the shape of a circle, snowshoe, or teardrop. A web with an opening in the centre was woven inside the frame. Plant cordage (plant fibres twisted together) or sinew (made from animal tendons) was used to form the web. It was customary to hang feathers from it, often from an owl or eagle, as a sign of breath or air.

There are several variations to the origin of the dream catcher. One legend of the Ojibwe Nation speaks of a tribe member named Asibikaashi, who busily wove dream catchers. She made them for all the new babies in the tribe. They were hung over their cradle boards so that they would have a peaceful sleep. When the Ojibwe Nation spread across the continent, Asibikaashi couldn't make the journey to provide all the new babies with a dream catcher, so the infant's mother, sisters, and grandmothers continued with the practice and tradition.

Another Ojibwe legend tells of a grandmother who was doing some sewing while a nearby spider was weaving a web. Her grandson came by, noticed the spider and was about to kill it, but the grandmother stopped him. When the boy left, the spider thanked the woman and provided her with a gift of gratitude. It was a magical web that allowed good dreams to be remembered and bad dreams to be trapped and forgotten.

The dream catcher was usually hung over a sleeping area and also where it would be exposed to the morning sun. Dreams were attracted to the web. The good dreams travelled through the centre hole of the dream catcher, slid down the feathers, into the thoughts of the sleeping individual. However, the bad dreams got entangled in the web and at daybreak, disintegrated with the light of the morning sun.

Although Native American dream catchers originated many years ago, they are now considered a safe haven above beds for dreamers of all ages and cultures.

A. Write "T" for the true sentences and "F" for the false ones.

1. _____ The dream catcher captures and saves good dreams.

2. _____ Asibikaashi made dream catchers for the infants in her tribe.

3. _____ One Native American legend tells of a grateful spider that left a magical web as a thank-you gift to the person who saved its life.

4. _____ Dream catchers were traditionally made from red maple wood.

5. _____ Feathers of an owl or eagle were hung from the dream catcher.

6. _____ Mothers, grandmothers, and sisters took over Asibikaashi's role of making dream catchers when Asibikaashi became too old to carry on.

7. _____ One material that was used in the dream catcher web was sinew, which was plant fibres twisted together.

B. Find three words in the passage for each syllable heading. Write two more of your own words under each heading as well.

One Syllable

Two Syllables

Three Syllables

Four Syllables

Five or More Syllables

Read the clues and complete the crossword puzzle with words from the passage.

Across

A. where one feels safe and secure

B. old and popular story

C. what people usually do

D. bad dreams

E. different forms

F. caught

Down

1. broken up, destroyed

2. people from whom you are descended

3. feeling grateful

D. Complete the chart below on adjective comparisons.

The **positive degree** is the base form of an adjective.
The **comparative degree** of an adjective compares two things.
The **superlative degree** compares more than two things.

	Positive	Comparative	Superlative
1.	sacred	more sacred	most sacred
2.	wise		
3.		more peaceful	
4.			best
5.	bad		
6.		safer	
7.			oldest
8.	busy		
9.		more magical	
10.			sleepiest

E. Record a journal entry of one of your dreams on the lines below. Include people, places, feelings, senses, and any associations that you can remember about your dream.

_____

_____

_____

_____

_____

_____

Bernoulli's Flying

Fluid is a substance with molecules flowing freely past each other. A fluid takes on the shape of its container. It can be a liquid or a gas.

A. George is reading a book about Daniel Bernoulli, one of the famous scientists. Help him fill in the blanks with the help of the words given.

> less   air   faster   slower   Bernoulli's   flight

In 1738, a scientist named Daniel Bernoulli discovered that

1._____ moving fluids exert 2._____ pressure on surfaces

that they are moving across than 3._____ moving fluids.

4._____ is a fluid.

It is Bernoulli's discovery, known as 5._____ Principle, that

allows for 6._____ to happen in the natural and man-made

world.

B. There are four forces acting on an airplane. Label the forces. Then answer the question.

1.   lift   drag
     thrust   weight

2.   Explain why the pictured airplane will lift upwards.

_____

_____

C. Complete the crossword puzzle.

lift aerodynamic housefly Bernoulli
streamlined drag thrust Houdini

Across

A. a forward-directed force

B. family name of a famous Swiss mathematician and scientist

C. a member of the group of the oldest known fliers in nature that is able to do a somersault and land upside down on a ceiling

D. a term describing a shape that offers minimum resistance to fluid flow

Down

1. the force that slows down a moving body

2. a word used to describe something that is designed with rounded edges so as to reduce drag

3. the force acting on an airfoil, opposing the force of gravity

4. name of the man who first flew an airplane solo in Australia

A. **Read the clues and complete the crossword puzzle on ancient Egypt.**

Across

A. written language used in ancient Egypt

B. an imaginary creature in the form of a human-headed lion

C. a jewellery piece to ward off evil

D. a structure with four triangular sides

Down

1. king of Egypt

2. the lifeline of Egypt

3. a preserved or embalmed body

4. a reed for making boats

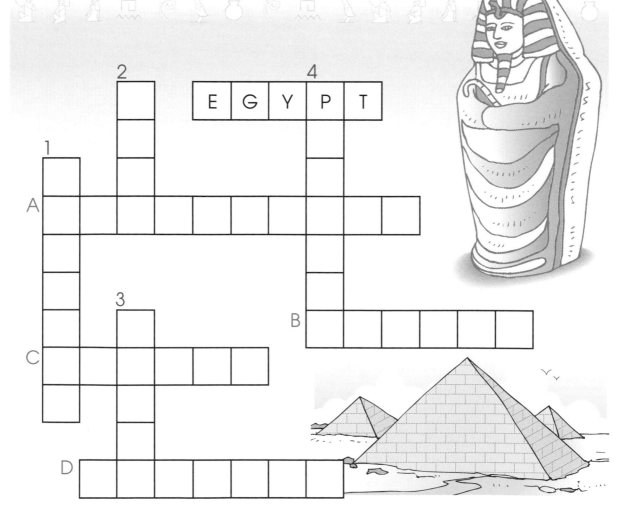

B. **Guess the meanings of the following Egyptian symbols. Write the representing letters.**

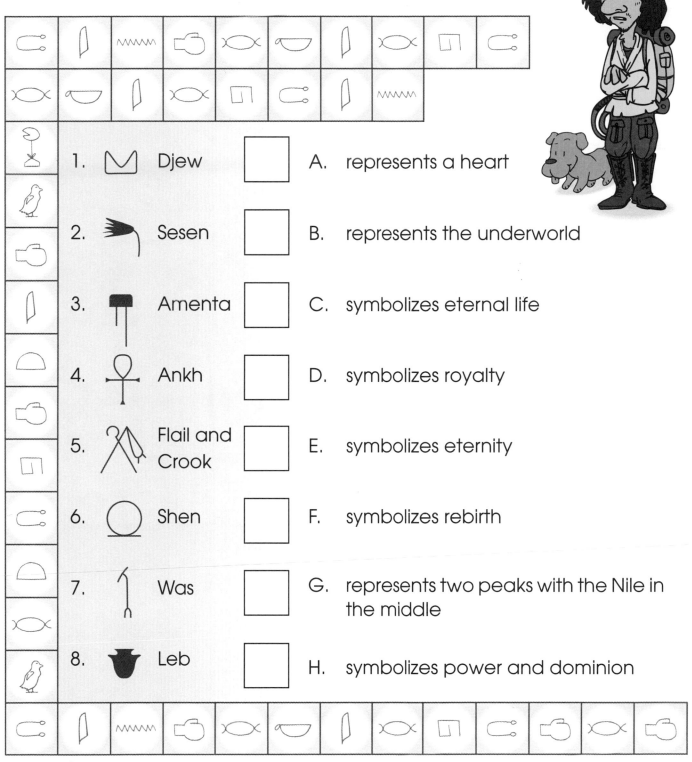

1. ᑌ Djew ☐   A. represents a heart

2. Sesen ☐   B. represents the underworld

3. Amenta ☐   C. symbolizes eternal life

4. Ankh ☐   D. symbolizes royalty

5. Flail and Crook ☐   E. symbolizes eternity

6. Shen ☐   F. symbolizes rebirth

7. Was ☐   G. represents two peaks with the Nile in the middle

8. Leb ☐   H. symbolizes power and dominion

Did you know? The ancient Egyptians believed that fried mice could cure toothache!

71

Ankh
Necklace

Materials:

- clay (see recipe)
- paint
- glaze
- brush
- cord or narrow ribbon
- sharp knife (Handle with care!)

Recipe – clay

- flour – 1 cup
- salt – 1 cup
- water
- cream of tartar (about 2 tablespoons)

Directions:

1. Mix clay as in recipe.
2. Shape an ankh using sharp knife. Let dry.
3. Paint the ankh. Add some patterns on the ankh. Let dry.
4. Paint with glaze. Let dry.
5. Thread through top of ankh with ribbon or cord.

A. Leo and his family visited Grandma last week. Look at the picture below. Help them solve the problems.

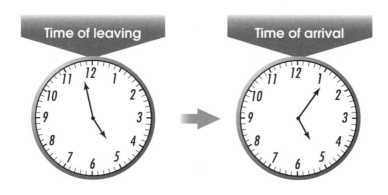

1. Write a decimal to show how far each place is away from Leo's house.

   Bakery _____ km   Theatre _____ km

   Library _____ km   Mall _____ km

   Hospital _____ km   Park _____ km

2. What is the distance between the park and Grandma's house? _____ km

3. What is the distance between the library and Grandma's house? _____ km

4. How far in metres is Leo's house away from Grandma's house? _____ m

5. Find the time it took Leo's family to travel from their house to Grandma's house.

Time of leaving		Time of arrival

   _____ min

6. How many metres did Leo's family travel in 1 minute? _____ m

B. **Leo and his sister, Celine, brought a lot of food to Grandma. Help them check ✔ the correct pictures.**

1. $\frac{1}{2}$ of the fruits were apples.

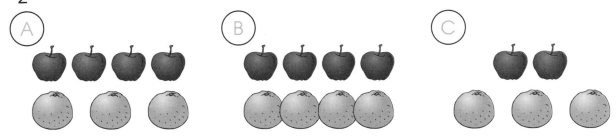

2. $1\frac{1}{4}$ boxes of muffins had chocolate chips.

3.   2 tenths and 4 hundredths kilogram of sunflower seeds

4.   1 and 47 hundredths kilograms of peanuts

75

C. Leo's family had a great time in Grandma's house. Help Leo record how much food was left in each container. Then solve the problems.

1.

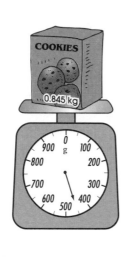
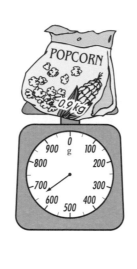

_____   _____   _____

2. How many grams of cookies did Leo's family eat?   _____ g

3. How many grams of popcorn did they eat?   _____ g

4. How many grams of chocolates did they eat?   _____ g

D. Write a fraction to solve each problem.

1. If Leo, Celine, and Grandma shared 16 cookies, each person would get _____ cookies.

2. If Leo, Celine, and their parents shared 39 grams of popcorn, each of them would get _____ grams of popcorn.

3. If Leo divided 26 pieces of chocolate into 5 groups, there would be _____ pieces of chocolate in 1 group.

E. **Grandma showed her needlework to her grandchildren. Help Grandma draw Xs from the line of symmetry on each cloth to complete the pattern.**

1.

2.

3.

4.

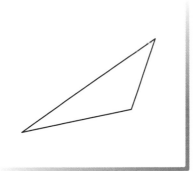 MATH GAME

Draw the rotation and reflection images in the boxes.

| Rotation Image | Reflection Image |

Mission Possible!

Imagine yourself being 320 000 kilometres from home, floating in outer space, with only one chance to make it home. This may sound inconceivable, but it did happen back in April 1970, with the mission of Apollo 13.

The Apollo 13 mission to the moon was progressing uneventfully until an oxygen tank exploded. James Lovell, the mission's commander, transmitted a now famous line to Mission Control in Houston, Texas – "Houston, we have a problem...". Their primary spacecraft, called Odyssey, was losing oxygen, power, and its ability to navigate. The trip to the moon's surface was cancelled and all efforts were being directed to bringing the astronauts home safely. People all over the world were concerned and began to follow the story.

The decision was made to abandon the Odyssey and all three astronauts, Lovell, Haise, and Swigert, moved into the Lunar Module (called Aquarius), the spacecraft built to land on the moon. The Lunar Module, however, was built for two people with supplies for two days. They were going to have to stay there for four days! Food, electricity, and oxygen needed to be conserved if they were going to make it home alive. The astronauts were crammed, the temperature dropped to 5°C, and moisture was condensing. Since the electrical systems were shut down, the astronauts could not use the navigation system so they had to navigate using the stars. One mistake could send them hurdling out into space, never to return. With their accurate star readings and their precision rocket burns, however, the astronauts managed to point Aquarius in the right direction – toward Earth.

The mission ended on April 17, 1970, with the safe splashdown of the capsule and crew into the Pacific Ocean.

A. **Read each question and skim the passage to find the answer. Write a brief answer on the line provided.**

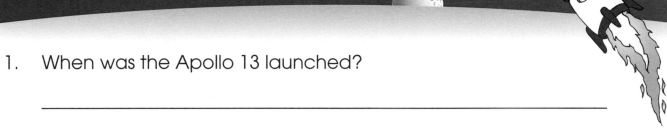

1. When was the Apollo 13 launched?

   _____

2. How many astronauts were aboard and what were their names?

   _____

3. How did they navigate once the electrical systems were shut down?

   _____

4. What problems did the astronauts face moving into the Lunar Module?

   _____

5. Why did the astronauts move into the Lunar Module?

   _____

6. Who was the mission commander for the Apollo 13?

   _____

7. Where was Mission Control located?

   _____

8. Why was the Apollo 13 mission aborted?

   _____

9. What was the Odyssey?

   _____

10. When and where did the capsule and crew land?

    _____

B.   Unscramble the words below. Use the clues given to help you.

1.   atingaev _____ (to direct on course)

2.   ocelnbciniave _____ (unthinkable)

3.   cnespiori _____ (exact measurement)

4.   novsecdre _____ (preserved)

5.   stenatmirtd _____ (passed on a message)

C.   Build two additional words for each root word by adding a suffix, a prefix, or both.

Some prefixes include: re, pre, dis, over, co, mis, con, in, and un

Some suffixes include: ful, ness, less, ish, able, ly, ance, est, and er

1.   conceive   _____   _____

2.   event   _____   _____

3.   happy   _____   _____

4.   hope   _____   _____

5.   appear   _____   _____

D.   Read each sentence. On the line, write "C" if it is a compound sentence and "CX" if it is a complex sentence.

1.   _____   Three days before the launch of the Apollo 13, Thomas K. Mattingly, command module pilot, was removed from the mission due to measles exposure.

2.   _____   Jack Swigert was Mattingly's backup and had only a few days of preparation before the launch.

3.   _____   Thomas K. Mattingly missed out on the Apollo 13 mission, but was able to fly on the Apollo 16 mission in 1972.

4. _____ Mattingly was not on the Apollo 13 spacecraft, but he was on the ground in a simulator, making every effort to figure out how the crew could safely re-enter the Earth's atmosphere without being incinerated.

5. _____ After the safe splashdown in the Pacific Ocean, the crew was escorted to the meeting site in Hawaii.

6. _____ While the astronauts were being transported to the meeting site, James Lovell's wife, Marilyn, and President Richard Nixon were waiting there to greet them.

E. Combine the following pairs of sentences to form complex sentences.

1. People all over the world learned about the aborted mission. They became gravely concerned about the safety of the crew.

_____

_____

2. The Apollo 13 mission was progressing smoothly. Then one of the oxygen tanks exploded.

_____

_____

3. The astronauts had to rely on the stars for navigation. The navigation system of their spacecraft did not function properly.

_____

_____

4. The Lunar Module was built for two people. All the three astronauts had to squeeze themselves into it.

_____

_____

Weather

A. **Read the rules and build the names of the clouds described.**

Rules to name a cloud

Shape: cumulus – meaning heaping
             stratus   – meaning layer or sheet

Height: cirro   – high (above 6000 m)
             alto   – middle (2000 m to 6000 m)
             No name is added to a low cloud.

*Nimbo (or nimbus) is added to the name of a cloud that brings rain.

cirrocumulus

cirrus

cumulonimbus

altostratus

cumulus

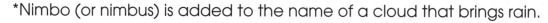

1. There's a fluffy cumulus cloud at the middle level of the sky.   _____

2. Fog covers the ground. Which cloud is it?   _____

3. A high, thin cloud covers the sky like a veil.   _____

4. Heaps of clouds have formed layers low in the sky. What is the formation?   _____

5. A stratus cloud is about 3000 metres above ground. What is it called?   _____

6. Cumulus clouds that are very high in the sky are sometimes called "mackerel" clouds. What are they?   _____

7. Dark, heaping rain clouds are bringing bad weather, maybe a thunderstorm.   _____

8. Low in the sky, they are piled up high.

   _____

9. More rain, but from a layer of grey cloud covering the sky

   _____

10. High in the sky, wispy, like feathers, not stratus or cumulus

    _____

Science Fun

A normal-sized cloud may weigh as much as a few elephants.

B. **The letters in each cloud form the answer to the question. Unscramble them and write the word on the line.**

1. Clouds are named according to their _____ and height in the atmosphere.

   p h a e s

2. Nimbo or nimbus refers to _____ bearing.

   a r n i

3. Puffy clouds, piled up and heaping are called _____ .

   u m u l u c s

4. Clouds in the middle part of the sky, not low and not high, have _____ added to their names.

   t o l a

5. Fog is really just a _____ cloud.

   a t r u s t s

6. We add the word _____ to a cloud that is very high.

   c i o r r

Roman Army

A. **Read about the Roman army and fill in the blanks with the words given.**

skills	roads	discipline	growth	tribunes
Capitoline	recruit	land	retirement	
Caesar	campaigns	army	citizens	Republic

The Roman army was responsible for the 1._____ of the Roman Empire. They were known for their 2._____ and 3._____ . In the days of the 4._____ , the army was made up of citizens who owned 5._____ .

One day a year, eligible Romans went to 6._____ Hill where the 7._____ chose the men for service. In the time of 8._____ , the army was reorganized. Romans were weary of the long 9._____ and it became difficult for the tribunes to 10._____ new soldiers. Near the end of 2 C.E., the army opened to include ordinary 11._____ . Even the poor were accepted. This was the beginning of a professional 12._____ in which men could serve until 13._____ .

Roman soldiers did not only fight. They also built 14._____ , aqueducts, and tunnels.

B. **Read the following statements about the Roman Empire. Write "T" for the true statements and "F" for the false ones.**

1. The Roman Empire spread over three continents. _____

2. The city of London was founded by the Romans. _____

3. The Romans discovered America. _____

4. Latin was the language of the Roman army. _____

5. The Roman Empire covered Egypt as well. _____

6. The Roman alphabet is still used in the western world. _____

7. Ancient Romans helped Greeks host the first Olympic Games. _____

8. The Roman law forms the basis of today's justice systems in the western world. _____

9. Augustus was the first emperor of the Roman Empire. _____

10. Gladiators were high-ranking soldiers. _____

11. There were no slaves in ancient Rome. _____

12. The Colosseum was where Romans listened to music. _____

13. The abacus was used for calculation. _____

14. Rich Romans hired Greeks to tutor their children. _____

Did you know? Lawyers in ancient Rome weren't allowed to charge fees, but they were allowed to receive gifts in return.

Materials:

dried beans   craft paint

xacto knife   aluminum foil

masking tape   paintbrush

craft spray (sealant)

2 oblong-shaped gourds

Gourd Maracas

Directions:

1. Cut hole in "bulb" part of gourd. Save the cut-out piece.

2. Scoop out pulp. Let dry overnight.

3. Pour 3 tablespoons of dried beans into gourd.

4. Cover the hole with aluminum foil.

5. Cover aluminum foil with the cut-out piece. Seal it with masking tape.

6. Paint gourd. Let dry.

7. Spray gourd with craft spray (sealant).

A. Mrs. Brown has a bakery. She uses a graph to show how many trays of muffins and doughnuts were sold in the past 9 months. Help her solve the problems.

Bakery

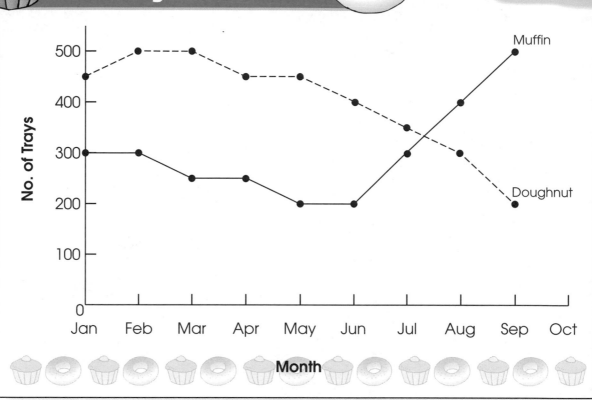

No. of Trays of Muffins and Doughnuts Sold

1. How many trays of muffins were sold in April? _____

2. How many trays of doughnuts were sold in August? _____

3. In which month did the bakery sell the most muffins? _____

4. In which month did the bakery sell the fewest doughnuts? _____

5. In how many months were the sales of muffins over 250 trays? _____

6. In how many months were the sales of doughnuts less than 300 trays? _____

MATHEMATICS

Week 7

B. **Mrs. Brown is talking with her son, Peter. Read what Mrs. Brown says and look at the graph in (A). Help Peter answer the questions.**

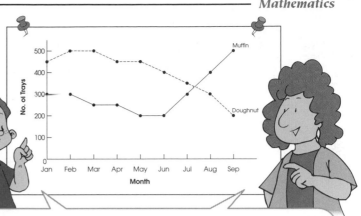

1. A famous doughnut shop was opened next to my bakery a few months ago. In which month do you think that shop was opened? Why?

_____

_____

2. I added a new flavour of muffin a few months ago. In which month do you think we started selling that muffin? Why?

_____

_____

3. If the sales of muffins follow the trend, how many trays of muffins will be sold in October?

_____

4. What was the average number of trays of muffins sold per month?

_____

5. What was the average number of trays of doughnuts sold per month?

_____

C. **The muffins sold in the bakery are in three different boxes. Help Mrs. Brown complete the table and solve the problems.**

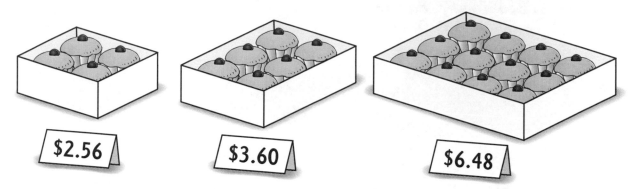

$2.56 $3.60 $6.48

1.

No. of 4-Muffin Boxes	1	2	3	4	5
No. of Muffins					
Cost					

2. On average, how much does a muffin cost in

   a. a box of 4? _____

   b. a box of 6? _____

   c. a box of 12? _____

3. Mr. Moxam wants to buy 10 muffins. How should he buy? How much does he need to pay?

4. If Mrs. Tino buys a box of 12 muffins instead of 3 boxes of 4 muffins, how much can she save?

D. **Mrs. Brown is making boxes to hold muffins. Help her put a check mark ✔ for the nets that can form boxes and cross out ✗ those that cannot. Then find the areas of the checked nets.**

1.
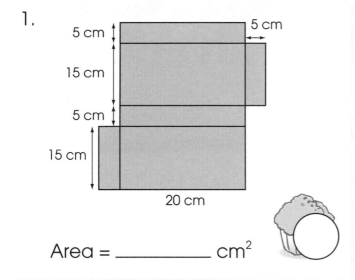

Area = _____ cm²

2.
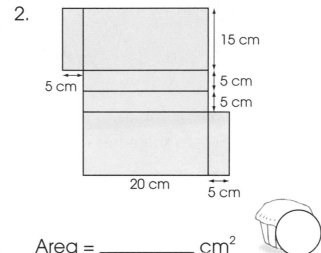

Area = _____ cm²

3.

Area = _____ cm²

4.

Area = _____ cm²

BRAIN TEASER

Help Freddie solve the problem.

Mrs. Brown pays Freddie $6 an hour for working in the bakery. If he works over 6 hours a day, he will get a $11.25 bonus. If Freddie earned $62.25 yesterday, how many hours did he work?

He worked _____ hours yesterday.

African Safari Adventure

Linda has just returned from a five-week safari adventure in Africa and is going to share her safari experiences with you.

Was there any special preparation before your trip? Of paramount importance was the medical preparation. I had a TB skin test, several vaccines, and anti-malaria medication. I also needed a passport. In addition, I purchased neutral-coloured and breathable clothing, a mosquito bed net, insect repellant, and leather hiking boots to protect against possible snakebites. I brought along binoculars and a camera too.

What parts of Africa did you see on safari? I saw parts of southern Africa, which included South Africa, Namibia, Botswana, and Zimbabwe.

Were there any times that you feared for your life? Probably the most frightening experience I had was while staying in a game reserve in the savannah of Botswana. I noticed that my tent had a large tear that had been repaired. After inquiring, I found out that the night before a lion had attempted to get in the tent. The camp manager assured me that safety precautions were in place. They gave me a whistle and a horn. I was instructed to sound the horn in case of a medical emergency and the whistle for any animal threat. I was told not to get the two confused. That night I didn't sleep at all.

Did you see any animals feeding on their prey? Did it bother you? During the night game drives, I did see a number of animals feasting on their prey. More disturbing however, was witnessing the actual kill of a wildebeest by a pride of lions.

What were your favourite animals to see? I was intrigued with the elephants in Zimbabwe. Their family ties go beyond life itself, as they will mourn the death of family members. The family gather together, stroking the body with their trunks, and covering it with clumps of soil and grass. It reminds me so much of human behaviour.

A. **Check ✔ the things that Linda did during her five-week safari adventure.**

1. Linda was taken to a hospital to have a TB skin test.

2. She stayed in a game reserve in Botswana.

3. She repaired a tent that had been damaged by a pride of lions.

4. She saw a pride of lions killing a wildebeest.

5. She witnessed how zebras mourned a dying member.

6. She was almost killed by an elephant at night.

7. She stayed awake the night in the game reserve.

8. She visited Zimbabwe and South Africa.

B. **Write five more questions to ask Linda so that you could learn more about her adventure.**

1. _____

2. _____

3. _____

4. _____

5. _____

C. **Use the coloured letters to find out the location of the world's largest waterfall.**

1. synonym for courageous   ___ ___ ___ ___ ___

2. synonym for sick   ___ ___ ___

3. homophone for seen   ___ ___ ___ ___ ___

4. antonym for weak   ___ ___ ___ ___ ___ ___

5. antonym for lost   ___ ___ ___ ___

6. homophone for herd   ___ ___ ___ ___

7. antonym for shout   ___ ___ ___ ___ ___ ___ ___

8. homophone for plane   ___ ___ ___ ___ ___

9. synonym for cautious   ___ ___ ___ ___ ___ ___

10. antonym for vanish   ___ ___ ___ ___ ___ ___

11. synonym for sneaky   ___ ___

12. synonym for vacation   ___ ___ ___ ___ ___ ___ ___

13. homophone for paws   ___ ___ ___ ___ ___

The World's Largest Waterfall : _____

D. **Rewrite each sentence with correct punctuation, capital letters, and quotation marks.**

1. i believe linda remarked that the hippopotamus could be the most dangerous of all the wild animals in africa

_____

_____

_____

2. my time in africa was a life-changing and unforgettable experience added linda

    _____

    _____

3. what is amazing and ironic commented linda is that the namibian desert stretches right up to the coast where it meets the frigid atlantic ocean

    _____

    _____

E.   Imagine that you are a journalist. Using the interview information from Linda's safari trip, write an article for the local newspaper summarizing the highlights of her trip.

Daily Chronicle

_____

_____

_____

_____

_____

_____

_____

_____

_____

_____

Properties and Changes of
Matter and Materials

A. See how the item changes in each picture. Write "solid", "liquid", or "gas" to tell the state of matter. Then put a check mark ✔ or cross ✗ in the right places to complete the table.

A

after 2 hours

B

after 2 hours

gas

C

after 15 minutes

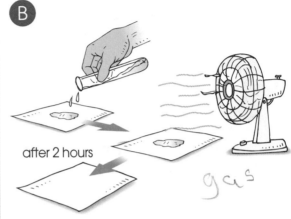

D

jello

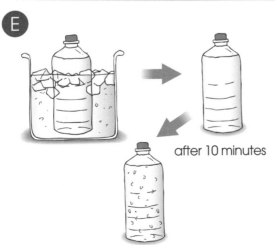

E

after 10 minutes

F

		State of Matter		Did the change involve a change of state?	Was the change reversible?
		Before	After		
1.	**A**				
2.	**B**				
3.	**C**				
4.	**D**				
5.	**E**				
6.	**F**				

B. **Fill in the blanks. Then write the coloured letters in order to complete what Michael says.**

1. Gas __ __ __ __ __ __ __ __ __ to form liquid.

2. Liquid __ __ __ __ __ __ __ __ __ __ to form gas.

3. Solid __ __ __ __ __ to form liquid.

4. Liquid __ __ __ __ __ __ __ to form solid.

5.

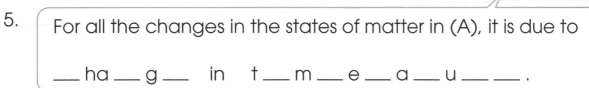

For all the changes in the states of matter in (A), it is due to

__ ha __ g __ in t __ m __ e __ a __ u __ __ .

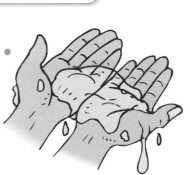

Try This! •

Make some "sol-quid", an unusual substance that
acts like both a solid and a liquid.

Mix 5 tbsp of corn starch with 3 tbsp of water.

Stir the mixture.

Poke it, roll it between your hands, and just let it sit on your palm.

How does it behave?

This can be pretty messy, so be prepared to clean up!

A. **Read about the early Chinese civilization and answer the questions that follow.**

The Chinese Civilization

China is an ancient country with written records dating back 4000 years. It was one of the four great ancient civilizations of the world, together with Egypt, Babylon, and India. China was one of the cradles of the human race. Fossils of the first Homo erectus, who lived 1.7 million years ago, were found in China.

Legend has it that the primitive tribes that lived along the Yellow River were unified into two tribes under the Yellow Emperor and the Fiery Emperor. They began to move southward about 5000 years ago. They conquered the tribes active in the southern part of China and the defeated tribes were incorporated into the tribes ruled by the Yellow and Fiery Emperors to become the Han people. This marked the beginning of the Chinese nation.

The earliest discoveries took place during this period. The Yellow Emperor invented the compass, which helped him win the battles against the southern tribes. His wife discovered silk by raising silkworms and made use of silk to produce the first garments. One of the Yellow Emperor's tribesmen by the name of Shen Nong tried and tasted various kinds of wild plants to identify herbs for curing disease. He was also able to select appropriate crops to be cultivated for food.

1. Why did the early tribesmen settle along the Yellow River?

   _____

2. Why was China considered a cradle of the human race?

   _____

3. Which ancient civilization mentioned no longer exists?

   _____

4. How did Shen Nong find suitable herbal medicine?

   _____

5. Name the two discoveries during the early tribal period in China.

   _____

B. **Refer to the Chinese numbers and try converting the Arabic numbers into Chinese numbers. The first one is done for you.**

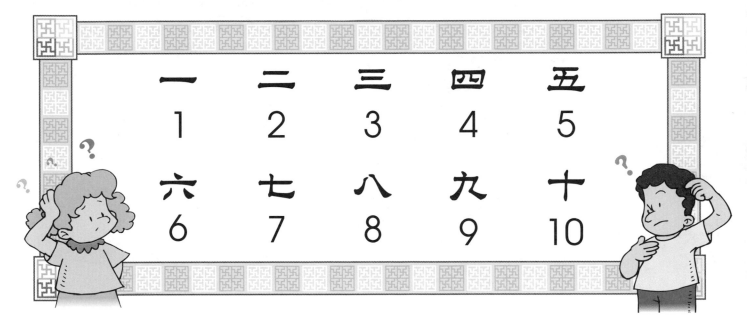

一	二	三	四	五
1	2	3	4	5
六	七	八	九	十
6	7	8	9	10

1. 11 __十一__   2. 50 _____   3. 38 _____

4. 18 _____   5. 24 _____   6. 70 _____

7. 59 _____   8. 33 _____

9. 63 _____

Did you know? China's four great inventions are the compass, papermaking, printing, and gunpowder.

Materials:

- white eggs
- paper towels
- darning needle
- food colouring
- vinegar (1 tablespoon per cup of water)
- bowl
- toothpicks
- water

Eggs-

-travaganza!

Directions:

1. Poke a hole in top and bottom of egg.

2. Blow into egg through one hole, pushing egg out through hole opposite. Let dry.

3. Mix food colouring, vinegar, and water in bowl.

4. Roll egg in colouring, vinegar, and water.

5. Lay on paper towels to dry.

6. Using toothpicks, dip into food colouring and "draw" on egg. Let dry.

MATHEMATICS

A. The toy shop owner, Mrs. Smith, stacks the empty cartons up to show the number of board games sold last week. Help Mrs. Smith complete the record.

Each carton holds 18 boxes of board games.

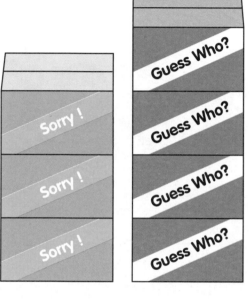

1. _6_ carton(s) or _108_ boxes of  were sold.

2. _3_ carton(s) or _____ boxes of  were sold.

3. _4_ carton(s) or _____ boxes of  were sold.

4. _1_ carton(s) or _____ boxes of  were sold.

5. Each box of cost $19.97. The total number of sold cost $ _____ .

6. On average, _____ boxes of board games were sold every day.

B. **Mrs. Smith uses different graphs to show the information about her toy shop. Look at the graphs and tell what mistakes she has made on the graphs.**

1.

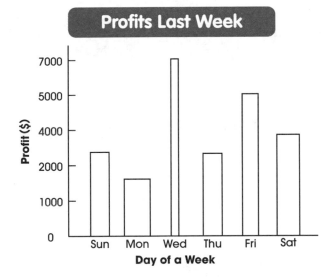

Profits Last Week

2.

Sales Last Week

$\bigcirc$ = $1000

Sun | Mon | Wed | Thu | Fri | Sat

3.

No. of Bags of Marbles Sold

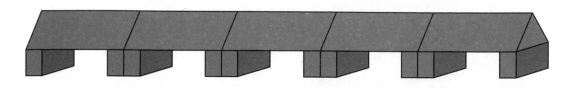

1.

Number of Groups	1	2	3	4	5	6
Number of 	1	2	3	4	5	6
Number of ▬	2	4	6	8	10	12

2. If there are 9 ◁▷, how many ▬ are there? _____ 18

3. If there are 24 ▬, how many ◁▷ are there? _____ 12

4. Write a rule that relates the number of ◁▷ to the number of ▬ .

   If there is 1 ▱ then there is 2 ▱

D. Complete the nets that can form the gift boxes. Then name the shapes of the gift boxes.

1.

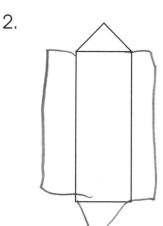

Prisme rectagle

2.

triangle prism

Week
8

MATHEMATICS

E. **Look at the pattern on the wrapping paper. Help Mrs. Smith complete the tiling patterns.**

1.

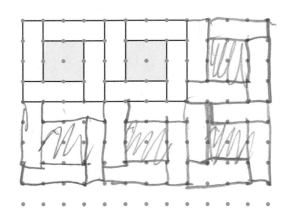

2.

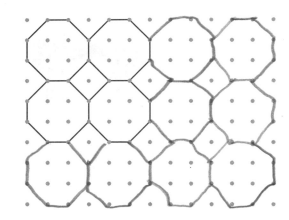

3.

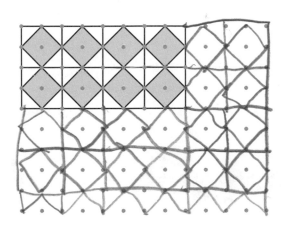

4.

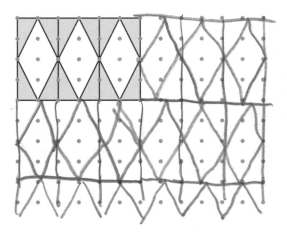

Use guess-and-test method to help Mrs. Smith solve the problem.

The cost of a box of puzzle and a box of building blocks is $54. If a box of puzzle is $8 cheaper than a box of building blocks, how much does a box of puzzle cost?

Cost of a Box of Puzzle ($)	22		
Cost of a Box of Building Blocks ($)			

A box of puzzle costs $ _____ .

Hillary's
Horrendous Holiday

Monday, July 7ᵗʰ

I was supposed to go away with my friend Laura to her family's luxurious cottage, but she got sick, so I am stuck going on another fun-filled camping trip with my parents and "lovely" little brother Leo. The drive was most enjoyable – crammed in the backseat beside Leo, listening to tedious toddler tunes in a monotone. We finally arrived at the campsite near dusk in the pouring rain and starved for dinner. Mom and Dad had purchased this new tent, which was supposedly easy to assemble. They were in way over their heads and were trying to read paper instructions in a downpour. After what seemed like an eternity, the tent was standing somewhat upright. I could have done it in a snap. Dad finally tried to light the portable stove so we could eat. More bad news – he forgot to pack the fuel. Dinner consisted of cereal in the backseat of the car, where we at least stayed dry.

Tuesday, July 8ᵗʰ

Well, at least the sun shone today. Mom and Dad finished unpacking, while I was the entertainment committee for Leo. I am so exhausted from playing "Hide and Go Seek" and "Ring Around the Rosie". Later I had some time to check out the facilities. What facilities – there were none! No shower, no electricity, and no toilets, just offensive odoured outhouses. At least I have my battery-powered CD player. Mom said that tonight we would be going out for dinner. I was elated, but then I found out afterward that what she meant was we were eating outdoors. Mom tried to help with the barbecuing, but Dad's the real expert. Let's just say we had real charbroiled burgers.

Wednesday, July 9ᵗʰ

Today, we drove to a beach. The fact that we were the only ones at the beach should have spoken volumes. The water was freezing, the beach was covered in seaweed, and there were swarms of deer flies. I knew this was as close to having a shower as I would get, so I braved the waters. I was horrified when I got out to find two leeches latched to my leg. Fortunately, Mom and Dad had a packet of salt in the car, which helped to remove them. I wonder what exceptionally exciting experiences tomorrow will bring?

A. **Find five alliterative phrases in Hillary's journal entries and write them on the lines below.**

> **Alliteration** *is two or more words in a group of words that begin with the same letter.*

1. _____

2. _____

3. _____

4. _____

5. _____

B. **Choose four letters from the alphabet to make up your own alliterative phrases of five words each. Circle each alliterative word.**

For example: (cutting) (cubes) of (crunchy) (carrots) (carefully)

1. _____

2. _____

3. _____

4. _____

C. **Hillary uses sarcasm throughout her journal entries. Find two sarcastic phrases and write them on the lines provided. Under each, write what Hillary was really meaning.**

> **Sarcasm** *is language with a mocking tone that means the opposite of what is being said.*

1. Sarcasm: _____

   Meaning: _____

2. Sarcasm: _____

   Meaning: _____

D. **Try rewriting these sentences using sarcasm.**

1. The trip was just so boring and exhausting.

   _____

2. He put me in a room so small that I could hardly lie straight.

   _____

3. The dish was the worst I'd ever tasted!

   _____

4. It just makes me look stupid wearing this pair of baggy pants.

   _____

5. Here comes a hyperactive and naughty child that no one likes to play with.

   _____

   _____

E. **Write a journal entry about Hillary's fourth day on her camping trip. Remember to date the entry and include her day's events, thoughts, and feelings.**

ENGLISH

F. Read the clues and complete the crossword puzzle with words from the passage.

Across

A. lasting forever

B. something built to serve a purpose

C. blood-sucking water worms

D. same tone of voice

E. unpleasant to the senses

Down

1. very happy

2. more than ordinary necessities

3. tiresome and boring

4. degree of loudness

5. put together

6. horrible

7. drained of energy

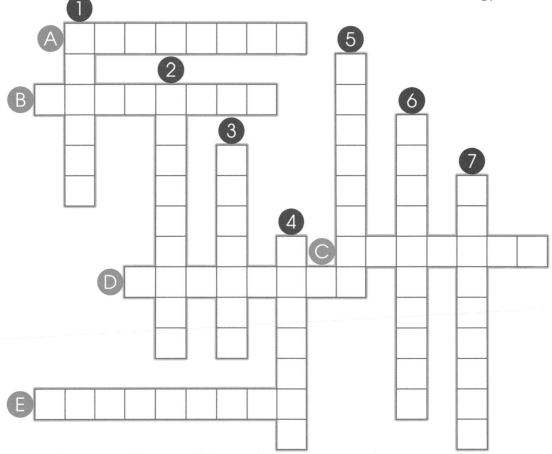

The SOLAR System

A. Read the verse and answer the questions.

Mercury, Venus
Earth and Mars
They're small, they're rocky
They're close to our star

Jupiter, Saturn
Past the Asteroid Belt
Uranus, Neptune
All gaseous, it's felt

Small or large
Rocky or gaseous
Those are the planets
That orbit the sun

1. Which planets are rocky?

_____

2. Which planets are gaseous?

_____

3. Which planets are part of the inner solar system?

_____

4. Which planets are part of the outer solar system?

_____

5. What else orbits the sun?

_____

Week
8

SCIENCE

B. **Read the information about the sun and the moon. Write "Sun" for the fact about the sun and "Moon" for the fact about the moon.**

1. Its gravitational pull is the major cause of the Earth's tides. _____

2. It orbits the Earth. _____

3. The Earth orbits it. _____

4. It reflects light. _____

5. It is the centre of the solar system. _____

6. Most planets have at least one. _____

7. It is terrestrial, or made of rock. _____

8. It has phases as seen from the Earth. _____

9. Its surface temperature is 6000°C. _____

10. Without it, there would be no life on the Earth. _____

11. When speaking about it, the word "lunar" is used. _____

12. When speaking about it, the word "solar" is used. _____

13. Human beings have landed manned spacecraft on it. _____

14. When struck by a meteor, a crater is left behind. _____

 # Sun and Moon
Trivia

- Of all the mass in our solar system, the sun contains 99%!

- You think the sun is hot? Lightning is 5 times hotter!

- People once believed that the sun orbited the Earth. We know now, it's the other way round.

Canada

Trivia Fun

???????? ?

Circle the correct answer for each question and see how well you know about Canada.

1. Which is the smallest province of Canada?

   A. Nova Scotia   B. Manitoba   (C.) Prince Edward Island

2. Which is the longest river in Canada?

   (A.) the Fraser   B. the Mackenzie   C. the St. Lawrence

3. Which animal is the national emblem of Canada?

   (A.) the beaver   B. the moose   C. the polar bear

4. Which city is the only walled city in North America?

   A. Quebec City   B. City of York   C. City of Vancouver

5. Which is the most populous province in Canada?

   (A.) Quebec   B. Ontario   (C.) British Columbia

6. Nunavut was established in 1999. What was the date?

   A. April 1   (B.) May 1   C. June 1

7. How many Great Lakes are there?

   A. 3   B. 4   C. 5

8. Where is Mount Logan, the highest mountain in Canada?

   A. Yukon   B. Newfoundland   C. British Columbia

9. Where do most of the Inuit people live?

   A. Yukon   B. Nunavut   C. Northwest Territories

10. In which year did "O Canada" become the national anthem?

    A. 1960   B. 1070   C. 1980

SOCIAL STUDIES

11. The CN Tower in Toronto was completed in ___ .

    A. 1965   B. 1975   C. 1985

12. Which sport was invented in Canada?

    A. bowling   B. baseball   C. hockey

13. Which of the following was invented in Canada?

    A. film   B. zipper   C. porcelain

14. The poppy is worn for ___ .

    A. Victoria Day   B. Canada Day   C. Remembrance Day

15. Which is the biggest island in Canada?

    A. Baffin Island   B. Vancouver Island   C. Prince Edward Island

16. Which is the highest waterfall in Canada?

    A. Delta Falls   B. Victoria Falls   C. Niagara Falls

17. Canada produces the most ___ in the world.

    A. copper   B. iron   C. zinc

18. The maple leaf has been a symbol of Canada since the ___ .

    A. 1700s   B. 1800s   C. 1900s

19. Which one of the following is NOT a Canadian?

    A. Wayne Gretzky   B. Glen Campbell   C. Michael J. Fox

20. The driest region on record in Canada is around ___ .

    A. Arctic Bay   B. Hudson   C. The Rockies

21. The richest dinosaur fossil find is in ___ .

    A. Ontario   B. Manitoba   C. Alberta

Materials:

- round balloon
- scissors
- water (half cup)
- pastel-coloured yarn
- glue (half cup)

Easter Basket

Directions:

1.   Blow up balloon.

2.   Cut yarn into lengths about 30 cm long.

3.   Mix glue and water (half cup to half cup).

4.   Dip yarn into glue and water mixture.

5.   Drape yarn around bottom of balloon in various directions, using different colours.

6.   Cover balloon until yarn is criss-crossing, leaving small spaces in between. Let dry for a couple of days.

7.   Break balloon and pull out.

ANSWERS

Week 1

Mathematics

A. 1. 14.6 ; 30° ; 75° ; 75° ; isosceles
   2. 10.41 ; 35° ; 90° ; 55° ; scalene
   3. 8.55 ; 60° ; 60° ; 60° ; equilateral

B. 1. A : 0.05   B : 0.2
      C : 0.3   D : 0.45
      E : 0.55   F : 0.7
      G : 0.8   H : 0.95
   2. 0.15 m
   3. 0.35 m
   4. 4
   5. Every 2 neighbouring flowers are 0.15 m apart and then 0.1 m apart alternately.

C. (Suggested answers)

   1. $\dfrac{12}{16}$; $\dfrac{3}{4}$ 2. $\dfrac{8}{20}$; $\dfrac{2}{5}$

   3. $\dfrac{16}{24}$; $\dfrac{2}{3}$

D. 1. ; $\dfrac{1}{4}$

   2. ; $\dfrac{1}{2}$

   3. ; $\dfrac{1}{2}$

E. 1. 96   2. 432
   3. 230   4. 410
   5. 425   6. 128.25

Math Game

B

English

A. 1. F   2. O   3. F
   4. O   5. F   6. F
   7. F   8. O

B. (Suggested answers)
   1. extremely
   2. presented
   3. gloomy
   4. great
   5. things
   6. gone beyond

C. 1. dreams
   2. industries
   3. lives
   4. werewolves
   5. benches
   6. dormitories
   7. alleys
   8. classes
   9. potions
   10. corridors
   11. countries
   12. reviews

D. (Individual questions)

E. groan ; through ; aloud ; stare ; coarse ; right ; one ; mourning ; whether ; our ; which ; band

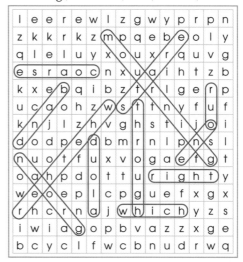

Science

A. Check pictures A, B, and F.

B. 1. I   2. C   3. C
   4. C   5. I

C. 1. bulb   2. cell
   3. wire   4. switch
   5.

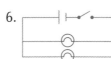

   6.

D. 1. series   2. parallel
   3. series   4. parallel

Social Studies

A. (Individual colouring)
   1. Northwest Territories
   2. Nunavut
   3. Newfoundland and Labrador
   4. Yukon

118

5. Saskatchewan
6. Quebec
7. British Columbia
8. Alberta
9. Manitoba
10. Ontario
11. Prince Edward Island
12. Nova Scotia
13. New Brunswick

B. (Individual writing)

Week 2

Mathematics

A. 1. 3.40 ; 3 ; 40
   2. 5.70 ; 5 and 70 hundredths
   3. 1.90 ; 1 and 90 hundredths
   4. 5.10 ; 5 and 10 hundredths
   5. 0.60 ; 60 hundredths
   6. 4.20 ; 4 and 20 hundredths
   7. 7.80 ; 7 and 80 hundredths
   8. $11.20
   9. $17.50
   10. $28.70
   11. $4.10
   12. 5

B. 1. 472.03
   2. 179.55
   3. 89.26
   4. 305.77
   5. Camera ; Necklace
   6. 382.77
   7. 44.63

C. 1. $\frac{8}{12}$ $(\frac{2}{3})$ 2. $\frac{1}{12}$

   3. 0   4. $\frac{4}{12}$ $(\frac{1}{3})$

   5. a. $84.66   b. Benny's Store $10 OFF

D. 1. a. 1   b. 2
      c. 3   d. 4
      e. 5   f. 7
      g. 8   h. 9
      i. 10
   2. a. 1   b. 2
      c. 3   d. 4
      e. 5   f. 6
      g. 7   h. 8
      i. 9

Brain Teaser
190

English

A. 1. These became the first roller coasters.
   2. Many riders were injured.
   3. Amusement parks became popular.
   4. They had no money for leisure activities.
   5. Theme parks were opening again and different roller coaster designs were created.

B. 1. H   2. E
   3. A   4. F
   5. C   6. B
   7. G   8. D

C. 1. Circle : Cedar Point ; Six Flags Magic Mountain
      Underline : parks ; world
   2. Underline : cost ; roller coaster ; millions ; dollars
   3. Underline : principles ; roller coasters ; gravity
      Circle : Sir Isaac Newton
   4. Underline : ride
      Circle : Cedar Point ; Top Thrill Dragster ; May
   5. Circle : Six Flags Magic Mountain ; Scream ; Spring
      Underline : ride
   6. Circle : The Supreme Scream
      Underline : world ; rides ; storeys

D. (Suggested answers)
   1. The first roller coasters, which were called "scream machines", appeared in Russia in the 16th century.
   2. When the Great Depression struck in 1929, the amusement park industry was forced to close down.
   3. People enjoy riding on roller coasters because they derive a lot of excitement from the rides.

E. 1. C   2. A
   3. B   4. B
   5. A

F. (Individual writing)

Science

A. 1. sound
   2. light / electrical
   3. electrical / light
   4. heat
   5. chemical
   6. elastic
   7. kinetic
   8. gravitational

ANSWERS

B. 1. heat
   2. kinetic
   3. kinetic
   4. heat ; light
   5. kinetic ; heat

C. 1. chemical ; heat
   2. chemical ; heat

Social Studies

A. Legislative : Parliament – Senate ; House of Commons
   Executive : Sovereign ; Governor General ; Prime Minister ; Cabinet ; Ministries and Civil Service
   Judicial : Supreme Court – Federal Courts ; Provincial Courts

B. (Individual answers)

C. (Individual drawing and writing)

Week 3

Mathematics

A. A : 5.11   B : 4.09
   C : 4.76   D : 4.79
   E : 3.96   F : 5.21

B. 1. $9.97 \times 5 = 49.85$; 49.85
   2. $1.45 \times 3 = 4.35$; 4.35
   3. $12 \times 16 = 192$; 192
   4. $38 \times 12 = 456$; 456
   5. $885 + 1248 + 1682 = 3815$; 3815

C. 1. 90° ; 72° ; 120° ; 78°
   2. 60° ; 150° ; 90° ; 60°
   3. Hamburger, Pita, Sandwich, and Pizza
   4. Hamburger, Pie, Pizza, and Sandwich
   5. $\frac{90}{360}$ ($\frac{1}{4}$)   6. $\frac{60}{360}$ ($\frac{1}{6}$)

D.

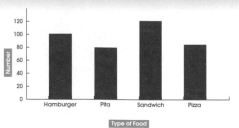

Food the Customers Got from Spinning Spinner A

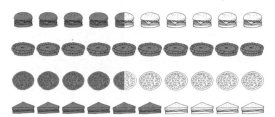

Food the Customers Got from Spinning Spinner B

Each picture = 10

Brain Teaser

127

English

A.

July 10

Dear Mom and Dad,

¶Adriana and I are having a fantastic time at Uncle Ross and Aunt Joyce's. It is like a paradise here, with an overlooking view of the water called "Satellite Channel" (not the television kind, Dad). ¶I'm learning to have a real appreciation for wildlife and the outdoors. Yesterday, while on route on the charter plane from Vancouver to Victoria, we were amazed to spot a pod of approximately 20 orcas, their dorsal fins piercing the water each time they surfaced. It was an incredible sight! Did you know that pods of the resident killer whales are made up of the mother's immediate and extended family members? They may stay together as a family even after they're fully grown and can live anywhere from 50 to 80 years. ¶Today, we saw a number of sea lions and otters frolicking in the water. It seemed quite peculiar to see this one otter lying on its back; it had a stone on its belly and a scallop in its paw. We discovered afterward that otters actually float on their backs while they crack open the seashell of their prey with a rock. ¶You won't believe this – there's a pair of bald eagles nesting in Aunt Joyce and Uncle Ross's very own backyard. It's astounding to see the eagles swooping in at speeds of up to 160 kilometres per hour over the water for their daily fish catch. The term "eagle eyes" is no joke. They can spot fish at distances of about 1.5 km away. ¶Aunt Joyce doesn't mind the eagles hanging out in their fir trees, but she does get frustrated with the deer and rabbits that frequent their grounds. These sneaky vegetarians arrive after dusk, having already eaten their main meal in nearby fields, only to enjoy Aunt Joyce's roses and lilies for their dessert. I guess they feel comfortable trespassing on the property, since there is no dog to frighten them off. ¶Tomorrow, Uncle Ross is taking us on an excursion to Johnstone Strait, where he's confident that we will sight a pod or two of orcas. Apparently in July and August, the number of whales in this area peaks, due to salmon passing through (one of their favourite foods). They naturally make this one of their main foraging territories. I'll give you more details when I get home.

Love,
Nicole
P.S. Adriana is a bit homesick.

B. 1. F   2. F
   3. F   4. O
   5. O   6. F
   7. F   8. O

C. 1. She saw a pod of approximately 20 orcas.
   2. She saw two bald eagles spot fish at great distances.
   3. They were the deer and rabbits that frequented Uncle Ross and Aunt Joyce's grounds.
   4. "They" refers to orcas and "this" refers to Johnstone Strait.

D.

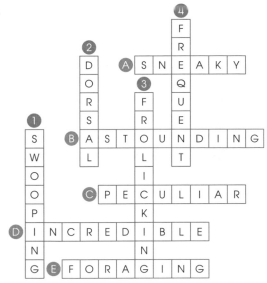

E. 1. A   2. P
   3. A   4. P
   5. P   6. A

F. 1. A big fish was spotted by the bald eagle.
   2. We were taken to the shore by Uncle Ross in his van.
   3. Nicole and Adriana saw a pod of orcas.
   4. The warden reminded us to be careful.
   5. A hearty meal was prepared for us by Aunt Joyce.

Science

A.

B. 1. Newton
   2. Torque
   3. spoke
   4. inclined plane
C. (Individual design)

Social Studies

A.

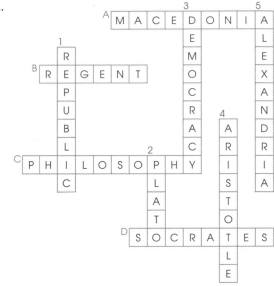

B. 1. Athens is named for Athena, the goddess of wisdom.
   2. Greeks took over Attica in 1900 B.C. and the name became Athens.
   3. Athens defeated Persia and became an empire.

Week 4

Mathematics

A. 1. 275 ; 175 ; 225   2. 300
   3. 275 ; 300 ; 300   4. 8

B. 1. a.    b. $\dfrac{45}{100}$; 0.45

   2. a.   b. $\dfrac{40}{100}$; 0.40 (0.4)

C. (Suggested answers for "Coloured Part")
   1. E : 10 ; $\dfrac{5}{10}$, $\dfrac{1}{2}$ L : 7 ; $\dfrac{4}{7}$, $\dfrac{8}{14}$

     I : 9 ; $\dfrac{4}{9}$, $\dfrac{8}{18}$ T : 7 ; $\dfrac{2}{7}$, $\dfrac{4}{14}$

     O : 12 ; $\dfrac{5}{12}$, $\dfrac{10}{24}$ N : 11 ; $\dfrac{6}{11}$, $\dfrac{12}{22}$

     Y : 7 ; $\dfrac{5}{7}$, $\dfrac{10}{14}$

2. 26   3. $\frac{13}{26}$ ($\frac{1}{2}$)

D. (Individual drawing of the congruent letters)
1. 45°   2. 115°
3. 60°   4. 130°

Brain Teaser

1. $\frac{1}{4}$ 2. 90

3. $\frac{1}{3}$ 4. 120

5. 150

English

A. 1. Athletes in this sport perform daredevil aerial stunts while skidding onto and over obstacles at astonishing speeds.
2. His father founded the National Skateboarding Association.
3. It is two and a half rotations above the half-pipe.
4. (Any two of the following)
   • He is featured in commercials, films, and magazines.
   • He has his own signature video game and skateboard clothing line.
   • He interviews athletes and does commentary at skateboarding events.
   • He has established the Tony Hawk Foundation.
5. It helps subsidize the building of public skateboard parks across the United States.

B. 1. extreme   2. compete
3. stunts   4. ollie
5. obstacles   6. skateboard

C. Paragraph One : B
Paragraph Two : A
Paragraph Three : A
Paragraph Four : B
Paragraph Five : B

D. Action Verb : rotate, glide, applaud
Saying Verb : exclaim, whisper, ask
Thinking/Feeling Verb : wonder, believe, amaze

E. (Individual writing)

Science

A. Skeletal System : cartilage, bone, ligament
Circulatory System : capillary, vein, artery
Nervous System : cerebrum, cerebellum, optic nerve
Respiratory System : trachea, bronchiole, bronchus
Digestive System : gall bladder, salivary gland, esophagus

B. stomach ; spinal cord ; kidney ; muscle ; skin ; lung ; white blood cell

C. 1. 350   2. 5
3. 12   4. 46
5. 206   6. 72

Social Studies

A. 1. farming
2. specific
3. fields
4. cooking
5. home
6. 1200
7. traded
8. 500
9. temples
10. palaces
11. pyramids
12. mathematics
13. astronomy
14. hieroglyphics
15. archaeological
16. temples
17. tombs
18. Mexico
19. collapse
20. conflicts
21. climate
22. food

B. Two   ••   Three   •••   Four   ••••
Six   ▬•   Seven   ▬••   Eight   ▬•••
Nine   ▬••••   Eleven   ▬▬•   Twelve   ▬▬••
Thirteen   ▬▬•••   Fourteen   ▬▬••••   Fifteen   ▬▬▬
Sixteen   ▬▬▬•   Seventeen   ▬▬▬••
Eighteen   ▬▬▬•••   Nineteen   ▬▬▬••••

Challenge

(Individual answer)

Week 5

Mathematics

A. Board Game : 24.06
Puzzle : 25.50
Racing Car : 74.40
Laptop : 49.98
Teddy Bear : 15.49
Guitar : 22.98

B. 1. 100 − 25.50 − 25.50 = 49 ; 49
2. 80 − 24.06 − 49.98 = 5.96 ; 5.96
3. 100 − 74.40 − 15.49 = 10.11 ; 10.11
4. 22.98 − 19 = 3.98 ; 3.98

C. 1. B ; Cube ; 6 ; 8
2. D ; Rectangular prism ; 6 ; 8
3. C ; Triangular prism ; 5 ; 6
4. E ; Triangular pyramid or Tetrahedron ; 4 ; 4
5. A ; Rectangular pyramid ; 5 ; 5
D. 1. Bear (1,3) ; Yo-yo (5,2) ; Doll (8,0)
2. 1, right ; 3, up
3. 4, left ; 4, down

Math Game

6

English

A. 1. T
2. T
3. T
4. F
5. T
6. F
7. F
B. (Suggested answers and individual new words)
One Syllable : can, bad, red
Two Syllables : willow, circle, centre
Three Syllables : origin, continent, continued
Four Syllables : American, customary, variations
Five or More Syllables : Asibikaashi, disintegrated, originated
C.

D. 2. wiser ; wisest
3. peaceful ; most peaceful
4. good ; better
5. worse ; worst
6. safe ; safest
7. old ; older
8. busier ; busiest
9. magical ; most magical
10. sleepy ; sleepier
E. (Individual writing)

Science

A. 1. faster
2. less
3. slower
4. Air
5. Bernoulli's
6. flight
B. 1.

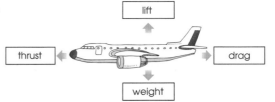

2. The shape of the wing causes the air moving over it to speed up more than the air going under it. The slower moving air under the wing exerts more pressure than the faster air moving air over it, and lift is produced. This difference in pressure pushes the airplane upwards.

C.

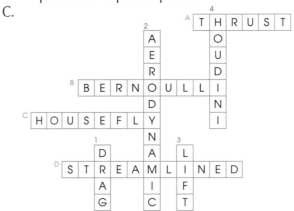

Social Studies

A.

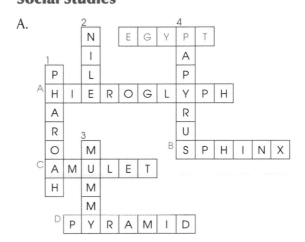

B. 1. G
2. F
3. B
4. C
5. D
6. E
7. H
8. A

ANSWERS

Week 6

Mathematics

A. 1. Bakery : 0.9   Theatre : 1.6
     Library : 2.3   Mall : 3.5
     Hospital : 4.7   Park : 5.4
   2. 0.6   3. 3.7
   4. 6000   5. 8
   6. 750

B. 1. B   2. C
   3. A   4. B

C. 1. 450 g ; 650 g ; 1210 g
   2. 395   3. 250
   4. 370

D. 1. $5\frac{1}{3}$ 2. $9\frac{3}{4}$

   3. $5\frac{1}{5}$

E. 1.   2.

   3.   4.

Math Game

(Suggested drawings)

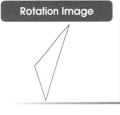

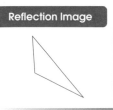

English

A. 1. In April 1970
   2. Three : Lovell, Haise, and Swigert
   3. Using the stars
   4. It was built for only two people with supplies for two days.
   5. Their spacecraft was losing oxygen, power, and its ability to navigate.
   6. James Lovell
   7. In Houston, Texas
   8. An oxygen tank exploded.
   9. The primary spacecraft
   10. On April 17, 1970 in the Pacific Ocean

B. 1. navigate
   2. inconceivable
   3. precision
   4. conserved
   5. transmitted

C. (Suggested answers)
   1. conceivable ; inconceivable
   2. uneventful ; uneventfully
   3. unhappy ; happiness
   4. hopeful ; hopeless
   5. disappear ; appearance

D. 1. CX   2. C
   3. C   4. C
   5. CX   6. CX

E. (Suggested answers)
   1. When people all over the world learned about the aborted mission, they became gravely concerned about the safety of the crew.
   2. The Apollo 13 mission was progressing smoothly until one of the oxygen tanks exploded.
   3. Since the navigation system of their spacecraft did not function properly, the astronauts had to rely on the stars for navigation.
   4. The Lunar Module was built for two people, so all the three astronauts had to squeeze themselves into it.

Science

A. 1. Altocumulus
   2. Stratus
   3. Cirrostratus
   4. Stratocumulus
   5. Altostratus
   6. Cirrocumulus
   7. Cumulonimbus
   8. Cumulus
   9. Nimbostratus
   10. Cirrus

B. 1. shape   2. rain
   3. cumulus   4. alto
   5. stratus   6. cirro

Social Studies

A. 1. growth   2. skills
   3. discipline   4. Republic
   5. land   6. Capitoline
   7. tribunes   8. Caesar
   9. campaigns   10. recruit

11. citizens   12. army
13. retirement   14. roads
B. 1. T   2. T
    3. F   4. T
    5. T   6. T
    7. F   8. T
    9. T   10. F
    11. F   12. F
    13. T   14. T

Week 7

Mathematics

A. 1. 250 trays
    2. 300 trays
    3. September
    4. September
    5. 5 months
    6. 1 month
B. 1. In May. Because the sale of doughnuts has been decreasing since May.
    2. In June. Because the sale of muffins has been increasing since June.
    3. 600 trays of muffins will be sold in October.
    4. The average number of trays of muffins sold per month was 300.
    5. The average number of trays of doughnuts sold per month was 400.
C. 1. No. of Muffins : 4 ; 8 ; 12 ; 16 ; 20
       Cost : $2.56 ; $5.12 ; $7.68 ; $10.24 ; $12.80
    2. a. $0.64   b. $0.60   c. $0.54
    3. He should buy a box of 4 muffins and a box of 6 muffins.
       He needs to pay : $2.56 + $3.60 = $6.16
       He needs to pay $6.16.
    4. She can save : $2.56 x 3 – $6.48 = $1.20
       She can save $1.20.
D. 1. ✔ ; 950   3. ✔ ; 550

Brain Teaser

8.5

English

A. 1.   2. ✔
    3.   4. ✔
    5.   6.
    7. ✔   8. ✔
B. (Individual writing)
C. 1. brave   2. ill
    3. scene   4. strong

5. found   6. heard
7. whisper   8. plain
9. careful   10. appear
11. sly   12. holiday
13. pause
Victoria Falls

D. 1. "I believe," Linda remarked, "that the hippopotamus could be the most dangerous of all the wild animals in Africa."
    2. "My time in Africa was a life-changing and unforgettable experience," added Linda.
    3. "What is amazing and ironic," commented Linda, "is that the Namibian Desert stretches right up to the coast where it meets the frigid Atlantic Ocean."
E. (Individual writing)

Science

A. 1. liquid ; solid ; ✔ ; ✔
    2. liquid ; gas ; ✔ ; ✗
    3. solid ; solid ; ✗ ; ✗
    4. solid ; liquid ; ✔ ; ✔
    5. gas ; liquid ; ✔ ; ✔
    6. liquid ; solid ; ✔ ; ✗
B. 1. condenses
    2. evaporates
    3. melts
    4. freezes
    5. change in temperature

Social Studies

A. 1. For travelling and cultivation
    2. Fossils of early men were found in China.
    3. Babylon
    4. He tried and tasted it.
    5. Silk and herbs
B. 2. 五十   3. 三十八
    4. 十八   5. 二十四
    6. 七十   7. 五十九
    8. 三十三   9. 六十三

Week 8

Mathematics

A. 1. 6 ; 108   2. 3 ; 54
    3. 4 ; 72   4. 1 ; 18
    5. 359.46   6. 36

B. (Suggested answers)
  1. The vertical scale is wrong. The width of the bars is not uniform. The spacing of the bars is not uniform. Tuesday is missing.
  2. The size of the pictures is not uniform. The pictures do not align. A row should not begin with a half-picture. The 2 half-pictures are different. Tuesday is missing.
  3. The vertical scale is wrong. Dots are not joined with straight lines. Dots are not joined sequentially. Dots are not marked correctly to the days.

C. 1. 3 ; 4 ; 5 ; 6 ;
     6 ; 8 ; 10 ; 12
  2. 18
  3. 12
  4. The number of equals 2 times the number of  .

D. (Suggested drawings)
  1.   2.

  Rectangular prism   Triangular prism

E. 1.   2.

  3.   4.

Brain Teaser

(Individual guessing)
23

English

A. 1. "lovely" little brother Leo
  2. tedious toddler tunes
  3. offensive odoured outhouses
  4. leeches latched to my leg
  5. exceptionally exciting experiences
B. (Individual writing)
C. (Suggested answers)
  1. The drive was most enjoyable.
     The drive was annoying.
  2. Dad's the real expert.
     Dad's the worst cook.
D. (Individual writing)

E. (Individual writing)
F.

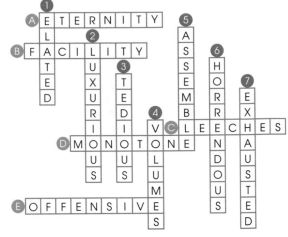

Science

A. 1. Mercury, Venus, Earth, and Mars
  2. Jupiter, Saturn, Uranus, and Neptune
  3. Mercury, Venus, Earth, and Mars
  4. Jupiter, Saturn, Uranus, and Neptune
  5. The Asteroid Belt

B. 1. Moon   2. Moon
   3. Sun   4. Moon
   5. Sun   6. Moon
   7. Moon   8. Moon
   9. Sun   10. Sun
  11. Moon   12. Sun
  13. Moon   14. Moon

Social Studies

  1. C   2. B
  3. A   4. A
  5. B   6. A
  7. C   8. A
  9. B   10. C
 11. B   12. A
 13. B   14. C
 15. A   16. C
 17. C   18. A
 19. B   20. A
 21. C

Dynamic Designs

Follow the patterns to draw lines to join the dots. Write your name on the lines. Cut them out and glue them on your folders.

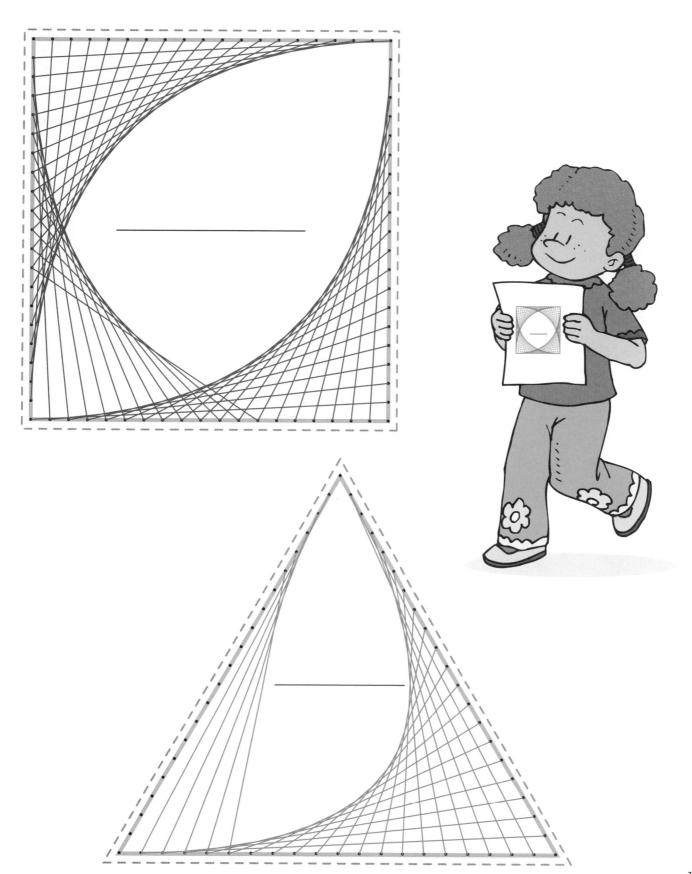

Pattern:

1 – 8
2 – 9
3 – 10
4 – 11
⋮
37 – 44
38 – 1
39 – 2
40 – 3
41 – 4
42 – 5
43 – 6
44 – 7

Make your own pattern.

Pattern:

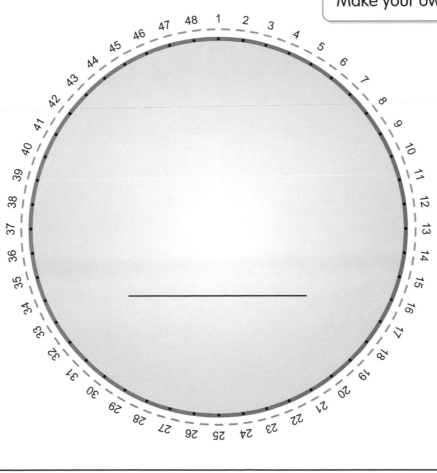

Compound Word Makers

Draw eight pictures that can form four compound words in the boxes on page 133. Cut out the pieces on this page and page 133.

2 or more players

Place the pieces face down. Each player takes turns to draw two pieces. Keep the pieces if the pictures can form a compound word. If not, place the pieces back in the pool. When all the pieces are drawn, the players show their pictures and say the compound words. The one with the most compound words wins.

Answers:

sunflower ; desktop ; firefly ; firecrackers ; starfish ; cupboard ; cupcake ; keyboard ; goldfish ; honeycomb ; nutcrackers ; pancake ; toothbrush ; eggshell

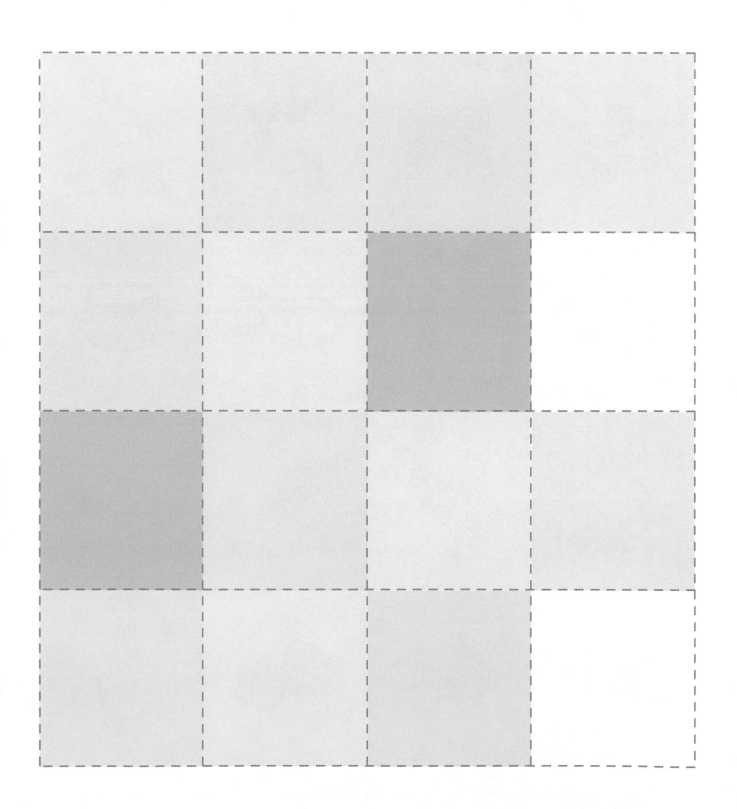

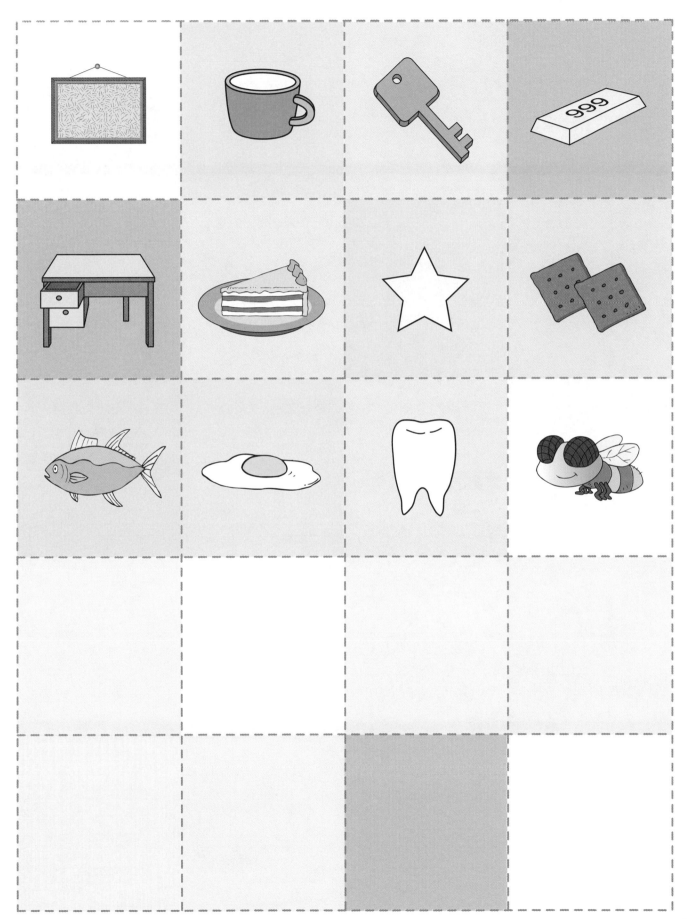

Cut out the boards. Then play with your friend to see who completes the game first.

2 players

Instructions:

Write digits from 1 to 9 in the blank boxes. Every row, column, or 3 x 3 square must contain all the nine digits.

LEVEL 1

	6				4	5		
8			5	1		4	6	
	1	4		2	3	8		9
1			4	5	8		3	
	9		7		6			
		5	2	9	1	6		8
6		7	1	8			9	
	4	2		6	5			1
3		1	9			2	5	

	6				4	5		
8			5	1		4	6	
	1	4		2	3	8		9
1			4	5	8		3	
	9		7		6			
		5	2	9	1	6		8
6		7	1	8			9	
	4	2		6	5			1
3		1	9			2	5	

Answers:

2	6	9	8	7	4	5	1	3
8	7	3	5	1	9	4	6	2
5	1	4	6	2	3	8	7	9
1	2	6	4	5	8	9	3	7
4	9	8	7	3	6	1	2	5
7	3	5	2	9	1	6	4	8
6	5	7	1	8	2	3	9	4
9	4	2	3	6	5	7	8	1
3	8	1	9	4	7	2	5	6

LEVEL **2**

6	1		9	7			3	
	5	7	3	1				4
	3				2			
3								6
9	7	2	6		3	8	4	1
1								7
			2				8	
5				9	7	1	6	
	2			3	5		7	9

6	1		9	7			3	
	5	7	3	1				4
	3				2			
3								6
9	7	2	6		3	8	4	1
1								7
			2				8	
5				9	7	1	6	
	2			3	5		7	9

Answers:

6	1	8	9	7	4	2	3	5
2	5	7	3	1	8	6	9	4
4	3	9	5	6	2	7	1	8
3	8	4	7	2	1	9	5	6
9	7	2	6	5	3	8	4	1
1	6	5	4	8	9	3	2	7
7	9	1	2	4	6	5	8	3
5	4	3	8	9	7	1	6	2
8	2	6	1	3	5	4	7	9

Cut out the pictures and place them face down. Ask your friend to pick three pictures for you to make up a funny story. After that, it's your turn to pick three pictures for your friend.

Funny Pyramids

Cut out and glue the nets of the pyramids.

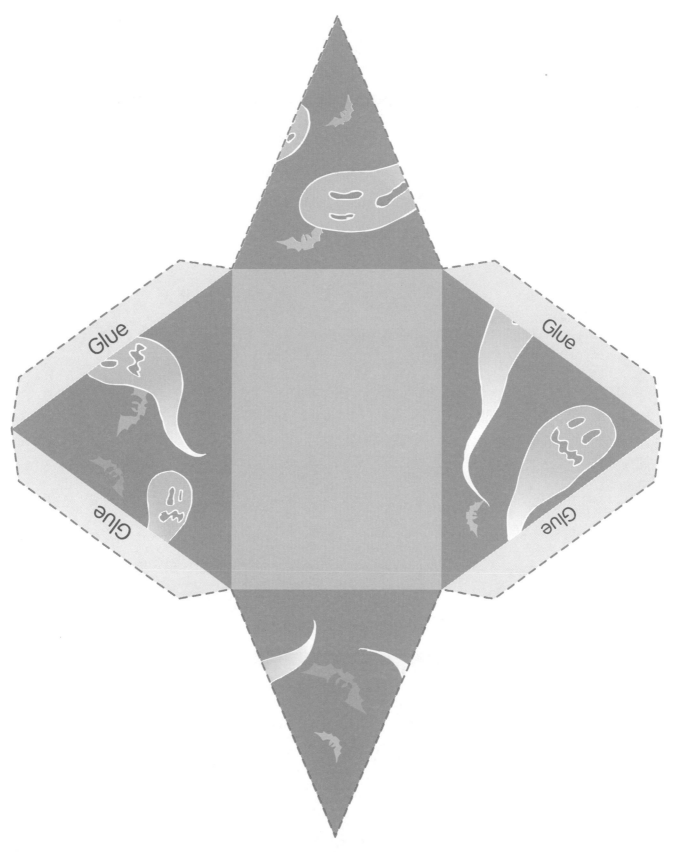

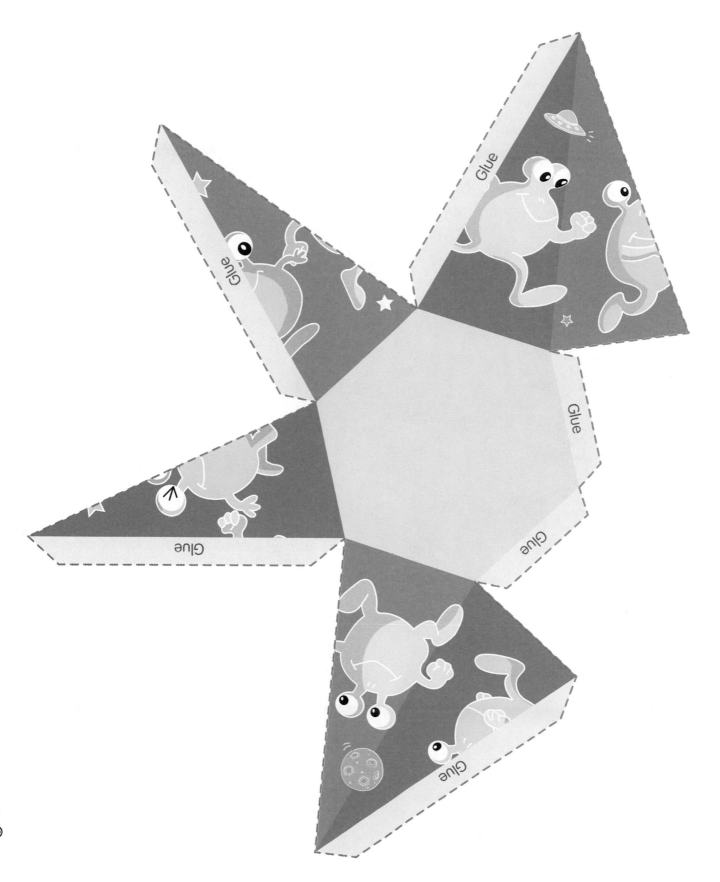